ENı

MW01258203

"Dr. Fisher's book provides ı
detours forced on the healthcare
Washington, but also a way out. Dr. Fisher is the personification of the
word "indefatigable" and outlines the important role Health Savings
Accounts can play, a subject the reader will find he has mastered."

> Keith Smith, M.D., Diplomate-ABA
> *Co-Founder and Director, Surgery Center of Oklahoma*
> *Co-Founder, Free Market Medicine Association*

"In this very informative and readable work, Dr. Fisher has succinctly
outlined why an ideologically driven approach to American health care
policy, which has proceeded for decades while willfully ignoring economic
facts, has brought us to the current crisis situation. This is a problem for all
Americans.

"This work should be required reading for all students of American
health care policy, physicians and patients alike."

> Richard A. Armstrong, M.D., FACS
> *A strong advocate of patient-directed care, has served on the boards*
> *of several healthcare organizations including Docs4Patient Care*
> *Foundation and as a contributor to the American College of Surgeons.*
> *Recognized as a national authority he has testified in Congress as an*
> *advocate for the importance of the patient-physician relationship.*

"In order to fix the broken American health care system, one must
truly understand how we broke it. This book is an important read for
those seeking to understand the problem. In his book, Dr. Fisher does an
excellent deep dive into the history of American medicine. He effectively
describes the rise of organized medicine and the injection of the Federal
government into health care. He clearly defines the efforts of modern organized medicine and federalized health care's struggle to maintain control,
while spiraling out of control. He completes this journey by proposing
thoughtful patient-centered solutions that build upon ideas introduced in
our co-authored prescient piece written many years ago in the Washington
Times. It is very well done."

> Lee S. Gross, M.D., Board Certified, Family Medicine
> *President, Docs 4 Patient Care Foundation*
> Co-Founder, Epiphany Health Direct Primary Care

"*Understanding Healthcare a historical perspective* is aptly named. Dr. Fisher's book provides an essential survey of 150 years of U.S. healthcare policies, without which it is impossible to properly evaluate the cause of our current challenges, or to forge effective, lasting, and equitable solutions. A must read for all those who care about the future of American medicine."

Beth Haynes, M.D., FAAFP
Executive Director, Benjamin Rush Institute

"Ken Fisher's perspective on healthcare is a veritable treasure. Besides being a gifted writer who is able to speak to even a nonmedical audience, Dr. Fisher has a keen awareness of the historical factors that have led us to where we are in healthcare today and understands a potential way out."

Marion Mass, M.D., Board Certified, Pediatrics
Cofounder and Executive Vice President of Practicing Physicians of America. She is a practicing pediatrician, wife and mother.

Understanding Healthcare:
a historical perspective

by

Kenneth A. Fisher, M.D.

Understanding Healthcare
a historical perspective

© 2016 by Kenneth A. Fisher

Published by Freedom in Health Care
4335 Roxbury Lane, Kalamazoo, MI 49008

ISBN-13: 978-0-9971511-2-1

Book design and cover by Keith Everett Jones

Dedication & Acknowledgements

*This book is dedicated to the concept
that to understand how to create
a far superior healthcare system in the U.S.
we must have knowledge of how and why
we have reached this dysfunctional state.*

Acknowledgement

Thanks to my wife who read every version
of every chapter with a critical and helpful eye.

CONTENTS

INTRODUCTION

"The practice of medicine is an art, not a trade; a calling, not a business; a calling in which your heart will be exercised equally with your head."

Sir William Osler (1849–1919)
Aequanimitas: With other Addresses to Medical Students, Nurses and Practitioners of Medicine, 2nd ed. (Philadelphia: Blakiston, 1925), p. 386

For most of human history, physicians had few scientifically proven therapies to offer their patients. The scientific method of testing a hypothesis with observation and data analysis, perhaps man's greatest intellectual achievement, did not exist until the mid-sixteenth century. Physicians Nicolaus Copernicus (1473-1543) and Andreas Vesalius (1514-1564) were pioneers in developing this type of thinking. The value of intellectual inquiry was emphasized, as was the importance of the common man.

The scientific method attained credibility during the Enlightenment, in the 17th and 18th centuries. In 1798, Edward Jenner published his careful observations that by infecting individuals with cowpox, he protected them from the scourge of smallpox. In the 19th century, many other gifted individuals added to the scientific bases of medicine with advances that significantly relieved human suffering.

In the newly created United States, scientific medicine lagged behind Europe, and there was little demand for formal education as a requirement for becoming a medical practitioner. This changed in large part owing to the efforts of a young physician, Nathan Smith Davis, the founder of the American Medical Association (AMA). He worked tirelessly, and adroitly, mostly through the AMA, to improve medical training and standards so that physicians could better care for their patients. In its early years, the AMA experienced tremendous growth and influence as it fostered better training and skills among American physicians. And as the care of patients improved, so did the influence of medical societies.

During the nineteenth century, physicians had access to far less technology than is available today, but they had greater expertise in the *art* of medicine. They knew how to connect with patients in a personalized, caring manner; for their part, patients felt secure in revealing their most personal and intimate life stories. Physicians had to excel in taking patients' histories and administering physical exams in order to obtain information regarding pathology and disease, as today's radiological and laboratory aids in diagnosis were not yet available. A competent physician had to be able to synthesize all available information using relatively limited pathophysiological knowledge in order to arrive at a diagnosis and devise a therapeutic plan.

In the late nineteenth century, Sir William Osler was a recognized master of this style of medicine—and while chief of the medical service at Johns Hopkins Hospital, he wrote the then seminal work *The Principles and Practices of Medicine*.[1] This book came to the attention of John D. Rockefeller, who noted the acute need for more scientific knowledge in medicine and in 1901 founded the Rockefeller Institute for Medical Research (subsequently Rockefeller University), dedicated to expanding the scientific basis of medicine.[2] The AMA enthusiastically welcomed this advance, understanding that better medicine meant better health for the nation as well as greater physician prestige and income. The advent of radiology and antibiotics—along with the creation of additional medical research capabilities funded both privately and by government, especially after World War II—led to an explosion of scientific medical knowledge.

No matter how much science advances our knowledge of the mechanisms of disease, however, medicine remains an art, combining science with humanity to address each individual's specific needs. "As essential, as invaluable as was the study of specific diseases through close, scientific investigation," eloquently observed Dr. Oliver Wendell Holmes, "there had to be more to the physician's comprehension and approach. There had to be concern for and some understanding of the patient. Medicine was a science to be sure, but also an art, the noblest of arts."[3]

Along with improved treatment of diseases came a call for the nation to do its best to provide these benefits more equitably to all its citizens. It soon became evident that in every society, for a variety of reasons, there were many who could not afford access to this ever-improving medical care. In response, the Labor government in Great Britain after its 1946 electoral victory expanded upon the 1911 National Health Insurance Act, a government-controlled defined benefit plan, and created the National Health Service.[4]

In the United States, although health insurance as an employee benefit was greatly expanded during World War II, Congress voted in 1965 to provide health insurance to those over 65 and the poor via government-run programs (Medicare/Medicaid) rather than by payments to individuals. The AMA, as the national voice of physicians, initially resisted any centralized control and payment for medical care and opposed the creation of Medicare. It soon became evident, though, that funding by the federal government not only greatly increased access by the elderly to medical care, but also handsomely increased the income of physicians and medical institutions.

As costs for these programs have escalated beyond anyone's anticipation, however, various price control schemes have been initiated, but the programs' costs remain unsustainable—and the unintended consequence of these relatively unsuccessful cost-containing schemes has been a deterioration of the intimacy between patients and physicians. This has caused an increased reliance on a more technological, bureaucratic, and expensive style of medicine. Because Medicare is by far the largest health care payer, almost all private insurers follow its price-fixed payment schedule for physicians. As these payments have diminished in real dollar value, physician time with patients has decreased considerably. Medicare and Medicaid payments to hospitals have also diminished, in many instances to below cost, leading to compensation via increased payments from private insurers, which in turn is in part responsible for substantially larger premiums.

The great challenge for our society is to create the proper environment in which patients and physicians work together to provide excellent care for *all* Americans at a cost that does not crowd out other critical needs. Such a model would require that physicians utilize our ever-expanding scientific knowledge and technology wisely, conserving resources while maintaining skills of humane interaction, physical diagnosis, and integrative thinking.

1

The Beginnings of Modern Science and the Value of the Common Man

Introduction

Throughout human history there has been a tension between older beliefs regarding any given sphere of human activity and newer thinking derived from human reason, observation, and the scientific method. This conflict is still ongoing. In medicine there are those who refuse to vaccinate their children despite mountains of evidence establishing vaccination's safety and efficiency. Billions of dollars are spent annually on food supplements and alternative medicines without their having undergone rigorous testing. Human nature being what it is, there are also those with vested interests who have prospered under the established belief systems and predictably rise up to defend them; but there are also those with curiosity who are always observing and trying to understand reality. Eventually truth is impossible to suppress, and progress is made.

The development of the scientific method, as depicted in this Figure is to me the foundation of the modern world and perhaps man's greatest achievement.

The creation of a hypothesis to be tested reflects a combination of a deep knowledge of the subject, imagination, and the ability to ask questions that are both insightful and testable.*

* To recognize those who are most able and creative in this pursuit of scientific truth, Alfred Nobel, the creator of dynamite and holder of 355 patents, initiated the prestigious Nobel Prizes. I was fortunate and privileged during my Internal Medicine residency to work for Dr. Solomon A. Berson, Chief of Medicine at Mount Sinai Hospital in New York City, who along with physicist Dr. Rosalyn Yalow developed methods to measure minute quantities of protein hormones in the blood—work that was awarded a Nobel Prize in 1977, shortly after Dr. Berson's untimely death.[5] This work enabled the discovery and measurement of many critical biologically active substances present in our bodies at very low concentrations.

Unfortunately, in a majority of instances our media do not present newer scientific findings in the context of the scientific method. Background, if presented at all, is minimal; the hypothesis tested is almost never mentioned; the strengths and shortcomings of the data are rarely, if ever, described. Explaining how the results add to our understanding of the process being studied is usually given short shrift. As a result, the general public acquires a superficial understanding of science in general as well as of the specific topic being studied.

In this chapter, I describe the very beginnings of the scientific method—in Europe, during the Renaissance (approximately the fourteenth through seventeenth centuries, depending on the definition)—as it was applied by two gifted physicians—who were willing to use their careful observations and keen minds to challenge age-old thinking. At that time, however, advances in science redounded to the benefit of a privileged few: primarily royalty, academicians and the intelligentsia. The Enlightenment (approximately the late seventeenth and eighteenth centuries), otherwise known as the Age of Reason, brought forward the concept of the intrinsic worth of all people, not just the privileged few. Also during the Enlightenment, the idea emerged that through an honest market, economic prosperity and growth could relieve the abject poverty of most in the population. Chapter 2 describes how combining the scientific method and concern for the common man created the beginnings of modern medicine in the nineteenth century.

A New Beginning in the Sciences in Europe

Using observation and his imagination, Aristotle came to the conclusion that all heavenly bodies revolved around the earth. This was about the fourth century B.C.E. Then, in about in the first century C.E., a Greek philosopher and mathematician, Claudius Ptolemy, working in Alexandria, Egypt, refined the earlier model on the basis of several observations, but kept the main idea that the earth was the center of the then known heavens, with all bodies revolving around it. This was called the geocentric model of the universe, and it had remarkable staying power, lasting until the sixteenth century.[6] Although Aristotle and Ptolemy were not Christians, their idea of a geocentric universe was eagerly adopted by the early Catholic Church, as it accorded nicely with several biblical references, such as Psalms 93:1, 96:10, and 104:5; I Chronicles 16:30; and Ecclesiastes 1:5. In medicine, Galen (130-200

C.E.), the Greek physician to the Roman Emperor Marcus Aurelius, wrote a textbook on human anatomy that was regarded as definitive for centuries.

Newer concepts in the physical and biological sciences had to wait for about another thousand years. The collapse of the Western Roman Empire in 476 C.E.; constant warfare; and the devastation caused by the Bubonic plague, which killed approximately one-third of the population, severely limited intellectual activity in Europe for approximately 1000 years. The city-states of Northern Italy eventually emerged as the trading and commercial centers of the Mediterranean, led by merchants and bankers rather than religious figures. As their wealth accumulated, they became patrons of the arts and humanities and acquired a renewed interest in writings from the Arabic and ancient Greek worlds. Increasingly, humanists and philosophers from the failing Byzantine Empire immigrated to the universities in Padua, Bologna, and Pisa; and as their faculty grew, these universities attracted intellectuals from all over Europe. The history of the University of Padua, where both Nicolaus Copernicus and Andreas Vesalius studied, is an example of this growth and development.[7]

The year 1543 C.E. was a seminal year for the development of science in Europe. For centuries, the ideas of Aristotle and Galen had dominated the physical and biological sciences. In that same year: 1) Nicolaus Copernicus an astronomer as well as a physician, published *De revolutionibus orbium coelestium* (*On the Revolutions of the Celestial spheres*), proposing that the sun, not the earth, was the center of the then known universe; and 2) Andreas Vesalius, also a physician, published *De humani corporis fabrica libri septem* (*The Seven Books on the Structure of the Human Body*), which for the first time provided an accurate and elegant depiction of human anatomy.

Nicolaus Copernicus (1473–1543)

Nicolaus Copernicus was born into a wealthy family living in the border area between Prussia and Poland. His maternal uncle, Lucus Watzenrode the Younger, was elected Prince-Bishop of the province of Warmia in 1489 and was an active participant in the ruling class of Poland. Copernicus's father died when he was ten, and his uncle became his mentor and sponsor. His uncle funded and oversaw his education, pav-

Scientific method for experimentation

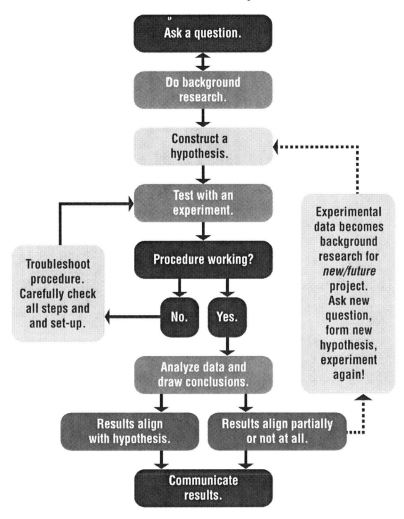

This diagram courtesy of Science Buddies - http://bit.ly/1GGMXYi

ing the way for him to become a canon of the church (a post just below Bishop, having responsibility for the cathedral and its financial holdings; canons also elected the Bishop), at the Frombork Cathedral. Being a canon assured Copernicus financial security for the remainder of his life. He lived his life as a loyal Polish citizen in Royal Prussia, which was a contested area between Poland and Prussia; the area at the time was under the rule of the King of Poland.

Copernicus attended two preparatory schools and then the University of Krakow, where he studied astronomy and mathematics; he was strongly attracted to the former and collected a large astronomy library. On the urging of his uncle in 1495, he left Krakow and studied Canon Law at Bologna University between 1496 and 1501. In Bologna he lived with Domenico Maria Novara, an astronomy professor who was seriously questioning Ptolemy's thousand-year-old concept of an earth-centered universe.[8] At this time, Copernicus was also seriously exposed to Greek humanities. He then entered the University of Padua (1501-1503, C.E.) to study medicine, but maintained his fascination with astronomy; even as he was studying medicine, he was formulating his hypothesis of a heliocentric universe. His uncle persuaded him to leave Padua after two years of a three-year medical degree program to obtain a doctorate in Canon Law at the University of Ferrara, after which he did not return to the Cathedral at Frombork, but rather to his uncle's castle in Lidzbark as secretary and physician. There he mingled with the ruling classes of Poland, attending the coronation of Polish kings and serving as a physician to nobility. As a canon of the church, he never married and had no children.

A true Renaissance man, Copernicus in 1507 published a translation from Greek to Latin of eighty-five poems by Thophylast Simocatta. In 1510, Copernicus, probably next in line to become bishop, left his uncle's castle and moved to Frombork so that while maintaining his responsibilities as a canon of the church, he could devote more time to his true passion, astronomical studies. Though in 1512 he published his own book of poems in Latin (Copernicus was an accomplished linguist, speaking Latin, Greek, Italian, German, and Polish), from 1512 to 1516 he was intensely involved in collecting more astronomical data, using whatever equipment he could, as the telescope had not yet been invented. Using the astrological tables of the time, Copernicus made many observations, collecting data while testing his hypothesis that the sun was the center of the solar system.

In 1514, Copernicus wrote an initial forty-page outline of his sun-centered theory, *Commentariolus*, but he resisted publication, instead sending copies to a few trusted friends. No doubt from this outline, however, the intellectual class knew Copernicus's theories of a sun-centered universe.

From 1516 to 1521 he was the economic administrator of the Provence of Warmia, publishing in 1517 a quantity theory of money that was used in both Poland and Prussia and is still taught to this day. In 1526 he published a treatise on the value of money, an early rendering of Gresham's Law that "bad money always chases out good money."

In 1533, Johann Widmanstetter, secretary to Pope Clement III, explained Copernicus's heliocentric system to the Pope; it was well received. In 1536, Cardinal Nikulaus von Schouder wrote to Copernicus from Rome, congratulating him on his fine work. In 1539 a young Protestant mathematician, Georg Joachim Rheticus from Germany, came to study with Copernicus. Rheticus encouraged Copernicus to publish his books on a heliocentric universe; he published an introduction to Copernicus's *Narratio Prima,* first *printed* in 1540, apparently convincing Copernicus to publish his full manuscript of *De humani corporis fabrica libri septem*, with Rheticus overseeing most of the printing in Nuremberg. The complete masterpiece was published in 1543, with a notation that an early copy had been presented to Copernicus just before his death in 1543. The treatise was dedicated to Pope Paul III.

After centuries of attempts to find the remains of Copernicus, they were found under the floor of the Frombork Cathedral in 2005. In 2009, using DNA technologies, samples from the skull were matched with the DNA from two strands of hair found in a manuscript written by Copernicus, located in Sweden.[9] (The manuscript was in Sweden because King Adolphus Augustus had removed valuables from Poland as he was attempting a conquest between 1625 and 1629.)

Copernicus's concept of a heliocentric universe initially aroused some turmoil, but the church did not ban it until 1616—and that ban lasted until 1744.[10] Because many Catholic and Protestant officials have in the past believed in the literal interpretations of several biblical passages, the idea of the earth not being the center of the solar system was contested for centuries.

Copernicus, an obvious creative genius, developed new thinking in literature, economics, and most importantly science through astronomy—because, among other things, he was not confined by previously accepted concepts. He was able to create a new hypothesis—a sun-centered solar system—, which he tested with his own, by today's standards, crude observational data.[11] Publishing his masterpiece shortly before his death in 1543, Copernicus participated in making that year the beginning of a period of sophisticated human inquiry in Europe that continues throughout the world to this day. He demonstrated that scientific inquiry is a continuously evolving process, always requiring new insights and refinement.

Andreas Vesalius *(1514–64 C.E.)*

Andreas Vesalius was born into a medical family in what is today southern Belgium. He attended the Catholic University of Leuven between 1529 and 1533 and then studied medicine at the University of Paris from 1533 to 1536. He subsequently returned to the Catholic University in Leuven where in 1537 he wrote a summary of the work of the tenth-century Arab physician Rhazon. He then matriculated at the University of Padua, which at the time had an excellent and progressive faculty with a strong tradition of human dissection. Upon receiving his M.D. degree from the University of Padua, he was immediately appointed a lecturer in surgery there, specializing in human anatomy. While instructing students, instead of continuing the tradition of having a novice demonstrate the actual dissection while the professor read verbatim from Galen's then available textbooks, Vesalius insisted on doing his own dissections.

Galen was the Greek physician to the Roman Emperor Marcus Aurelius. It is ironic that in the original Latin, Galen's instructions were for the dissections to be done by the students themselves. After the fall of Rome in 476 C.E., however, Galen's work was kept alive via translations into Arabic and was then followed in Bagdad and other major Arabic cities. In the twelfth century the Arabic version was translated back into Latin, the language of the learned in Europe, whereupon it became the foundation of European medicine. Unfortunately in the process of multiple translations, Galen's admonition for students to do their own anatomic dissections was lost.[12]

Vesalius visited the University of Bologna in 1540, and while doing his own dissections he found numerous errors in Galen's descriptions. It turned out that Galen's work was based on dissections of various animals, as dissecting humans was against the law in Rome. In 1542, Vesalius traveled to Venice to supervise the creation of woodcuts of his anatomical drawings by technicians in the famous painter Titian's studio. He took the completed woodcuts along with the supporting text to Basel, Switzerland, where the work was published in its entirety in 1543. His text was immediately recognized as a masterpiece that elegantly, extensively, and accurately depicted human anatomy.

At the age of 29 because of the excitement around the publication of his text, Vesalius was invited to Mainz to present his work to the Holy Roman Emperor Charles V and was retained as a physician to the royal family. In 1544 he relinquished his post at Padua, married Anne van Hamme, and traveled extensively in Europe in service of the Emperor. From 1553 to 1556, Vesalius spent most of his time in Brussels, building an extensive and lucrative medical practice. In 1556, Charles V abdicated the Spanish throne in favor of his son Philip II, who shortly thereafter appointed Vesalius a Count with a lifetime pension. In 1559, Vesalius traveled to Spain with his wife and young daughter to become a physician to the court; in 1564, he left Spain (his wife and daughter returning to Brussels) on a pilgrimage to Jerusalem, but he died in transit.

A Brief Review of the Enlightenment

The Age of Enlightenment[13] [14], or The Age of Reason, is generally considered to have occurred from the late seventeenth through the eighteenth centuries, but its impact on mankind was and is profound to this day. The thinkers of the Enlightenment proposed the idea that humans had reasoning ability and could use it to make a better world for all people, not just for the nobility or the intelligentsia, the privileged few. This thinking had roots in previous centuries as scholars rediscovered the thinkers of ancient Greece and Rome.

Probably one of the greatest events in human intellectual history occurred in 1632, when Galileo Galilei used careful observation, with the aid of the telescope he invented, to support the Copernican concept that the earth rotated around the sun and not the opposite, as the Church held. Although Galileo was forced by the Church to renounce his findings, his ideas were read by intellectuals throughout Europe, and helped better the scientific method of inquiry. According to this thinking, no knowledge is absolute, old beliefs with no basis in fact are discarded, and progress is always needed to confirm, refine, test and probe deeper into any proposed hypothesis. Over three hundred and fifty years later, astrophysicists using satellites, radio telescopes, and extremely sophisticated equipment that Copernicus and Galileo could never have imagined are continually expanding our knowledge of the universe.

In France, two immensely talented scholar/philosophers were busy expressing new ideas. One was Jean-Jacques Rousseau, an exponent of a conception of equality according to which individuals were sovereign and all deserving of an outstanding education. The American Colonial fathers built upon this concept, believing that for a democracy to thrive, its citizens must have the necessary education to govern themselves and to be productive members of society. The other was François-Marie Arouet, known by his nom de plume, Voltaire, an exponent of the ideas of freedom of religion and expression along with separation of church and state.

In London, John Locke, a physician and philosopher, was considered by many the original proponent of Classical Liberalism, whose ideas were the foundation of the American Declaration of Independence and of modern concepts of self and identity. Locke's thinking influenced many exponents of the Enlightenment, including Rousseau, Hume, and Kant. In Scotland, David Hume argued for the importance of searching for empirical information. Another Scotsman and great philosopher, Adam Smith, whose book, *An Inquiry into the Nature and Causes of the Wealth of Nations* (1776), is the foundation of modern economics, has had a major influence on the concept of building wealth through free markets in the modern nation-state.

In America, in order to unite against the British, the colonies agreed on the importance of spirituality, but not on a distinct religious order. Jefferson, Washington, Franklin, Paine, and others were greatly influenced by the Enlightenment, and by the concept of a Deist god (rejecting the supernatural, stressing ethical behavior).[15] To these men, the natural world and the existence of human reason were enough to believe in a God, without the trappings of organized religion.

As one might expect, there was a backlash against the new ideas of the Enlightenment. At the beginning of the nineteenth century, there was a strong reaction, sometimes coming under the designation of Romanticism, to the attempts to scientifically explain nature. This philosophy was in part a reaction to the overcrowding and poverty experienced by many as a result of the increasing industrialization of society, which also led to a sudden burst in European population.[16] The ensuing sense of alienation contributed to the feeling of a need to return to nature.

The desire to hold on to preconceived beliefs rather than explore the science behind the phenomena of the natural world is subscribed to by many to this day. In medicine, the struggle between long-held medical beliefs and the scientific discovery of the mechanisms of and possible cures for disease was part of the context of the progress made during the nineteenth century. The scientific inquiry into disease was based on the philosophy of the Enlightenment and the concept that human reason was vital if we are to understand the world we live in. The quest for scientific knowledge is an ever-evolving one, however, as such knowledge is not absolute and always needs further exploration.

2

Foundations of Modern Medicine: Advances in the 19ᵗʰ Century

Introduction

At the opening of the nineteenth century in the newly formed United States, most medicine followed the principles developed by the Salerno School of Medicine[17] over a thousand years ago. This was a belief system that had no foundation in science. It was based on the Four Elements that, according to ancient Greek teachings, made up the Universe: fire, air, water, and earth. In the human body, according to the Greek paradigm, blood represented fire, bile represented air, black bile represented water, phlegm represented earth. Disease occurred when these four elements were out of their proper balance—and the physician's duty was then to rebalance these four elements, thereby restoring the individual to health.

According to this philosophy of medicine, a competent physician had to be learned in the many varied combinations of these four elements and know just the right way to realign them.[18] The therapies used to achieve the "proper" balance, completely unproven for efficacy, were bleeding, purging, blistering, and Calomel, a toxic form of mercury.

This was a belief system passed on for centuries with no basis in fact; it was accepted with little questioning and with no experimental evidence. It also resulted in many physician-induced deaths - including that of George Washington, who in an attempt to cure his apparent epiglottis (a bacterial infection deep in his throat) underwent extensive bleeding, which culminated in his death in December 1799.[19] The acceptance of unverified doctrine was at the core of the Enlightenment's criticisms, setting the stage for the nineteenth-century establishment of the scientific basis of modern medicine. The process was slow and certainly not without controversy. As an example of public ambivalence toward medicine, in 1806 a New York medical licensing law favoring "learned physicians" was modified a year later to become unenforceable.[20] This in a microcosm defined the problem for state legislators and the public at that time: They wanted effective medicine, but because the science was lacking, all schools of thought were deemed equivalent.

There were some isolated instances of "modern" medical thinking before the nineteenth century, but it was that century that set the stage for medicine, as we know it today. What follows is not exhaustive, but is meant to give a flavor of the advances made during the nineteenth century, particularly the development of the scientific method, and why that century is regarded as laying the foundations of modern medicine.[21] Today it is accepted that new findings can change thinking on a subject, but this was not true in the early nineteenth century. What followed was that innovative and gifted men and women were overturning concepts and prejudices that had been revered for centuries.

Nineteenth-Century Medicine: We Walk on the Shoulders of Giants

A Scourge of Mankind: Smallpox

Smallpox, a viral disease, was one of the great killers throughout history. It is extremely contagious and is especially lethal amidst large numbers of uninfected individuals, as with armies. An early pioneer in abating smallpox in the *eighteenth* century was Lady Mary Wortley Montagu, who returned to England from Turkey with the idea of "variolation," taking a sample of smallpox material from a newly infected person and using it to deliberately inoculate an as yet uninfected individual. Variolation helped some, but caused serious disease in others; after initial acceptance, it quickly lost favor.[22] In spite of its dangers, however, to fight the threat of smallpox that was decimating his army, General Washington, under extreme duress, ordered variolation for all of his troops from 1777 to 1778.[23] Immunizing his troops caused minimal losses and was critical to the Continental Army's eventual victory. Imagine the difficulty of making a decision to deliberately lose some of your men in order to save most of them.

Then, *Edward Jenner (1749–1823)* appeared on the scene. He was a physician trained in London after having apprenticed at an early age and was greatly influenced by the ideas of the Enlightenment; he was also an amateur ornithologist. He made several careful observations and performed an experiment that under today's standards could never have been done.[24] Although he was unaware of the probable attenuation of the virus involved, he observed the following: Farm horses frequently became afflicted with a hoof disease which produced infected material, and individuals tending these horses frequently proceeded without hand washing to milking cows. Jenner observed that within a short period of time, pustules appeared on the cows' utters, and others milking the same cows developed pustules that resembled smallpox, but came down with a much milder disease. He then obtained some of the infected cowpox material from a milkmaid, Sarah Nelmes, and used it to inoculate a boy, James Phipps, who thereupon developed a mild case of cowpox; Jenner then inoculated the boy with smallpox material and found that he was completely immune.

Jenner repeated this process a number of times and with the same results before publishing his findings in 1798.[25] [26] This physician-ornithologist coined the term "vaccination" and became the father of modern immunology. His observations, and his discovery of a method of preventing death from smallpox, were initially ridiculed, especially by the clergy, but the advantages of vaccination quickly became evident, resulting in its wide acceptance. Many other successful vaccines followed in the nineteenth century: cholera in 1879, anthrax in 1881, rabies in 1882, tetanus and diphtheria in 1890, typhoid fever in 1896, and the first vaccine for plague in 1897.[27] These vaccines and those that followed are among the greatest gifts that medicine has bestowed on mankind. We in the twenty-first century have only a faint understanding of the devastation and misery these diseases caused in the past.

One of the pillars of medicine is physical diagnosis. This art was greatly improved when in 1816, *Rene Laennec (1781–1826)*, a physician and amateur flutist, made a startling discovery. While trying to examine the heart of a young stout woman in a Paris hospital, and with propriety demanding that he not directly put his hands on the lady's chest, he found that a rolled newspaper and later a hollow wooden tube applied directly to the woman's chest revealed magnified sounds of her heart, allowing for improved diagnosis. Laennec went on to discover that sounds emanating from the chest could also be helpful in better diagnosing lung physiology and pathology. This discovery greatly improved the art of physical diagnosis and led to the stethoscope, a tool that is used today by every physician throughout the world.[28]

For your physician to diagnose and understand your disease and to initiate a rational therapeutic plan, in most instances tissue must be obtained for pathological examination. This is also true of the autopsy necessary to determine the disease processes that caused death. No person is more responsible for modern pathology than *Rudolf Carl Virchow (1821-1902)*, an anthropologist, social activist, as well as an acclaimed physician and one of the founders of the effects of economic status on health. Virchow studied medicine and chemistry at the Prussian Military Academy from 1839 to 1843. He mastered the microscopy of human tissues and was influenced by the more scientific approaches to medicine originating in France and England even in his first job. Early in his career, he believed that clinical observation, animal experimentation, and microscopic pathological findings were the keys to understanding disease. Contrary to the accepted beliefs of the day, he believed that all cells emanate from other cells and that there was no such thing as spontaneous generation. This was critical to the development of a modern approach to biology and medicine.

Along with a colleague, Benno Reinhardt, Virchow founded a pathology journal now known as *Virchow's Archives*, an extremely influential publication. His thinking was original and differed from many of the accepted views of his time, but as the years passed, his genius became appreciated. He discovered that an abnormally large left supraclavicular lymph node is frequently the sign of a gastrointestinal malignancy, with the malignant cells carried to the node via lymphatic drainage. This finding is now known as "Virchow's node." Although normal clotting of blood after an injury or an open wound is beneficial, if blood clots spontaneously in an artery or vein, the clot may dislodge, causing damage, sometimes fatal, to tissues downstream. Virchow was a pioneer in the understanding of this process, called *thromboembolism*. Virchow also invented the liver probe, used to determine temperature at the examination time and thus approximate the *time* of death. This technique is frequently seen today on many mystery-oriented television programs.

As an anthropologist, Virchow studied skull measurements that debunked concepts of Aryan or any other European racial superiority. He would be thought of today as a believer in Western democratic liberalism. "Medicine, as a social science," he wrote, "as the science of human beings, has the obligation to point out problems and to attempt their theoretical solution: the politician, the practical anthropologist, must find the means for their actual solution. . . . The physicians are the natural attorneys of the poor and social problems fall to a large extent within their jurisdiction."[29]

As Virchow was revolutionizing pathology, surgeons were looking to expand their capabilities in fighting disease by being able to perform operations inside body cavities such as the chest and abdomen. They were limited, however, by the terrible pain caused by these procedures. What was needed was anesthesia, the ability to suppress pain either locally or by temporarily ceasing consciousness; this was one of the great advances of medicine. Anesthesia, along with infection control, opened the door to surgery, as we know it today. A sponge impregnated with a narcotic, or plant extracts of hyoscyamus or mandragora covering the nose and mouth to ease the pain of a procedure, were in use for centuries. They did not have the potency required, however, to enable surgery in a systematic manner inside body cavities.

Ether was first synthesized by Cordus in 1640; chemists knew of nitrous oxide, synthesized by Priestly in 1777; and chloroform was synthesized by Soubeiran in 1831, but ether's use as an anesthetic had to wait for about two hundred years.[30] Then in 1842, Dr. Crawford W. Long, a graduate of the University of Pennsylvania Medical School, used ether as an anesthetic for several minor surgical procedures.[31] He did not publish his findings, but his success became known through word of mouth. A few years later, in 1844, Dr. Horace Wells, a dentist, administered nitrous oxide first on himself and later on several patients. Dr. Wells tried to demonstrate his success during a surgical procedure performed by Dr. Warren at Harvard Medical School, but it was not successful. Another dentist, Dr. William T. G. Morton, used ether on a few patients and was successful; he demonstrated its potential in 1846, again with Dr. Warren (this time at Massachusetts General Hospital), in what is now known as "the ether dome." News of this success rapidly spread around the Western world, with Dr. Oliver Wendell Holmes giving it the name of anesthesia. Dr. James Simpson in Edinburgh preferred chloroform, which in the end proved more toxic than ether. Dr. John Snow successfully used chloroform in 1853 to facilitate childbirth in the case of Queen Victoria's eighth child, Prince Leopold.[32] Because of the Queen's status, church objections to the use of anesthesia in childbirth quickly ceased. For his part, Dr. Snow quickly became known as the father of anesthesiology as a result of his extensive studies describing anesthetic methods and agents.[33] Anesthesiology has greatly advanced since those early days, with the addition of many agents and a far better understanding of their mechanisms of action.

Dr. Snow was not done making seminal advances in medicine. His studies of cholera, a life-threatening massive diarrhea disease caused by the bacterium *Vibrio cholerae*, were groundbreaking. Cholera was and still is a problem for mankind, causing many fatal epidemics well into the twenty-first century.[34] John Snow, again before the discovery of the germ theory of disease by Louis Pasteur, used his powers of observation and reason to explain the cause of the infamous Broad Street cholera epidemic of 1854 in the Soho district of London. Applying both his powers of reason and his skepticism, Dr. Snow did not believe in the prevailing and accepted theory that epidemic diseases were somehow the result of "bad air," known as the miasma theory. He initially published his ideas on the spread of cholera in 1849 and again the year after his extensive investigations of the 1854 epidemic. He accumulated his own data on the epidemic by speaking to the families of those who died as well as those who were unaffected—and deduced that the water pump on Broad Street was responsible for the epidemic. Snow found that the company supplying the water to that pump had contamination from sewage; he thereby demonstrated a fecal-oral route of spreading the disease. Because of this work, John Snow is also known as the father of modern epidemiology.[35] An inspiration for all of us, Dr. Snow became a leader in his society not because of his status at birth, but rather because of his intellect, persistence, and hard work.[36]

But tragically, notwithstanding the beginnings of epidemiology, pathology, and anesthesia, patients were still dying after injuries, childbirth, and surgery. For centuries, childbirth, when assisted by physicians, was often associated with death from what was described as childbed fever (puerperal fever). Symptoms included lymphangitis (inflammation of lymphatic channels), phlebitis (inflammation of veins), pleurisy (inflammation of the lining over the lungs), pericarditis (inflammation of the sac surrounding the heart), and sometimes other complications. Today we would describe this as florid sepsis - infectious agents in the blood spreading to vital organs and, if unchecked, causing death. Unfortunately, the successes in decreasing puerperal fever by Charles White of England and the two Irish physicians Joseph Clark and Robert Collins—who practiced scrupulous cleanliness and conducted fewer vaginal exams during labor—were not followed. Even after Oliver Wendell Holmes (1809-94), the noted Paris-trained Boston physician, speculated in 1843 that puerperal fever was transmitted by those working in the maternity ward and published his thinking in an 1855 essay, "Puerperal Fever as a Private Pestilence," this theory was still ignored.[37] Then in 1861, *Ignaz Semmelweis (1818–65)* published, "The Etiology, Concept, and Prophylaxis of Childbed Fever," a study that took many years, and was based on careful observations and stringent cleansing techniques.[38] His approach was scientific and statistically sound and was accepted by some noted physicians and rejected by others. In actuality, Semmelweis may have been the first physician to have performed a statistically sound method of preventing infectious disease even before the germ theory of disease was discovered. Ironically, he died in an asylum after a mental breakdown caused by the very disease, sepsis, that he was so instrumental in defining.

Infectious agents, bacteria, fungi and viruses were responsible for the diseases that have always plagued mankind. The breakthrough in their science and treatment, the germ theory of disease, was the brainchild of the French chemist *Louis Pasteur (1822–95)*, one of the greatest medical thinkers of his or any time. His work provided the intellectual framework that explained the success of Semmelweis, Snow, and, shortly thereafter, Joseph Lister.[39][40] In 1856, Pasteur revealed that fermentation was caused by the growth of bacteria and that these bacteria had to be introduced into the broth, proving that there was no such thing as spontaneous generation. This work was the basis for the germ theory of disease. Pasteur demonstrated that microorganisms are responsible for the spoilage of beer, wine, and milk. Along with Claude Bernard, the father of modern physiology, whose independent investigations into endocrinology and liver function were themselves magnificent, Pasteur used mild heating to kill many of the noxious microorganisms present in these liquids by a process now known as pasteurization. He had the insight to propose that the same process of contamination of liquids was also responsible for the many diseases spread to patients owing to contamination. He understood that the natural barrier to microorganisms was the skin, and when its integrity is interrupted by trauma or by procedures performed by physicians, a portal of entry for pathogens was created. This explained the sepsis described by Semmelweis. Pasteur discovered that there were two types of bacteria, those that lived in an oxygen environment and those that preferred an environment without oxygen. Pasteur extended Jenner's work with smallpox vaccine by demonstrating that with anthrax, chicken cholera, and rabies, he could create protection against the disease by either subjecting the offending organism to chemical alteration or killing, before it was given to the patient. For these vaccines there was no need of an animal intermediary, as with Jenner's work with smallpox.

Across the Channel, a British surgeon, *Joseph Lister (1827–1912)*, who had observed that open (as opposed to closed) wounds often became infected, was convinced that the bacteria described by Pasteur were causing wound infections. Lister decided to try antisepsis, the killing of organisms, as opposed to asepsis—the prevention of contamination of organisms—, which is today's preferred method. He decided to apply repeated sprays of carbolic acid to the patient during the operation. He published his results in the *Lancet* in 1867, giving full credit to Pasteur's discoveries.[41] His concept of preventing bacterial growth in surgical wounds was initially received with mixed enthusiasm, and was practiced more in Europe than in the U.S. Physicians eventually accepted the concept, however, and now, to deal with possible contamination, aseptic techniques are standard practice.

Pasteur's work was expanded by *Robert Koch (1843-1910)*, a German physician who became the world's first microbiologist, and the father of modern bacteriology.

In 1876, Koch published proof that the *Bacillus anthracis* was the causative agent of anthrax. Along with his assistant Joseph Petri, Koch developed solid techniques of culture using the Petri Dish (glass or plastic dishes with covers filled with a gel like substance to promote bacterial growth) and he developed methods of staining which facilitated visualization of bacteria under the microscope. Koch isolated the bacteria that cause tuberculosis, cholera, typhus, tetanus, and plague, and he developed the four Koch's postulates, which are considered sufficient but not absolutely required to prove causation of infectious diseases.[42] Robert Koch was awarded the Nobel Prize in Physiology or Medicine in 1905. [43] [44]

---

4 Postulates

1. The microorganism or other pathogen must be present in all cases of the disease.

2. The pathogen can be isolated from the diseased host and grown in pure culture.

3. The pathogen from the pure culture must cause the disease when inoculated into a healthy, susceptible laboratory animal.

4. The pathogen must be re-isolated from the new host and shown to be the same as the originally inoculated pathogen.

Source: *University of Maryland, "Koch's Postulates to Identify the Causative Agent of an Infectious Disease".*

The lives of all people have greatly benefited from the understanding that infectious agents, bacteria, fungi, viruses, and parasites cause diseases that are frequently fatal. The significance of the pioneering work of Pasteur and Koch cannot be overestimated. It is inconceivable to practice medicine today without the armamentarium of modern anti-infectious drugs. (The first was penicillin, initially described by Alexander Fleming in 1928 and isolated by Howard Florey and Ernst Chain in 1938. All three were awarded the Nobel Prize in Physiology or Medicine in 1945.[45]) But resistance to these drugs is an increasing and serious problem. Tens of thousands of Americans are dying each year because of drug-resistant infections. Unfortunately, at this time, research into the development of new antibiotics that would be effective against these emerging highly resistant microorganisms is not as active as it should be. We must find ways to continue to increase our understanding of the molecular biology of these infectious agents so that new and effective drugs can be developed.[46]

Parasites, which through evolution have developed complex life cycles, have in the past caused serious human suffering and still do. The biggest killer is malaria. A pioneer in this field was Ronald Ross (1857–1932), a poet and mathematician as well as physician who dedicated his medical energies to eradicating malaria. His grandfather, Lt. Colonel Hugh Ross, suffered from the disease which ignited Ross's interest. He was awarded the Nobel Prize in Physiology or Medicine in 1902 for his 1897 discovery of finding the malaria parasite in the Anopheles mosquito after it had fed on a malarial patient's blood. He also demonstrated that he was able to transfer malaria from an infected bird to healthy birds via the blood feedings of a mosquito. This was proof that insects, as was suspected for centuries, were the vector (carrier or transmitter) of this disease.[47] [48] Although Ross's work took place over a hundred years ago; we are still fighting a battle with malaria. An effective vaccine against the parasite has so far eluded us, as has our ability to destroy the various mosquito vectors.[49]

Physicist *Wilhelm Conrad Roentgen (1845–1923)* the inventor of x-rays was responsible for creating an entirely new specialty, Radiology, a major advance in diagnostic studies. He received a degree in mechanical engineering from Polytechnic Institute in Zurich, Switzerland (now the Swiss Federal Institute of Technology, Zurich), and then a Ph.D. in physics from the University of Zurich in 1869. He quickly moved up the academic ranks, becoming Chairman of the Department of Physics at the University of Wurzburg.

Roentgen achieved almost instantaneous fame and became an overnight celebrity when on December 22, 1895 he demonstrated an x-ray photograph of his wife's hand. Roentgen had decided to study the effects of sending a powerful electric current through a gas of very low pressure enclosed in a tube excluding all light. He found that if he placed objects between the discharged rays from the tube and a photographic plate, the various densities of the object were revealed after developing the plate. First studied to examine the pathology of bones, x-rays were quickly adapted for diagnosis in other organs. Roentgen's pioneering work also led to the field of radiation oncology, applied in the treatment of various cancers. He was awarded the Nobel Prize in Physics in 1901.[50] Marrying Roentgen's techniques with today's computers and modern physics has led to the creation of CT (or CAT) scans and EMR diagnostic tools.

A much simpler but equally important diagnostic tool is the measurement of blood pressure. Considered one of the vital signs along with pulse rate and temperature, blood pressure, when either too low or too high, requires treatment. Facilitating its measurement was the work of Scipione Riva-Rocci (1863–1937), an internist and pediatrician who significantly improved the measurement of systolic blood pressure (the upper number) in 1896 with the use of a column of mercury connected by rubber tubing to an inflatable cuff around the patient's arm. This measurement, along with the later developed measurement of diastolic blood pressure, is standard in all physical examinations and important in determining health and longevity.[51] High blood pressure (hypertension), measured essentially this way, is a contributing factor in the development of many pathological processes, especially in modern societies.

Disease cannot be confined to physical ailments, however. Abnormal or pathological behavior can be equally if not more destructive to an individual, a community, or, in the case of tyrants, the world. An initial student of deranged behavior and the founder of a new branch of medicine, Psychiatry, was *Sigmund Freud (1856–1939)*. Freud was an excellent student, fluent in eight languages. He was an avid reader of Shakespeare in English throughout his life, and it has been speculated that Shakespeare's insights into human behavior, as manifested in the actions of the characters in his plays, had a profound effect on Freud's thinking. Freud graduated from medical school in 1881 and initially was successful pursuing a career as a research neurophysiologist. But in

1885, Freud, while on a fellowship in Paris, studied and learned hypnosis with the noted neurologist Jean-Martin Charcot. On returning to Vienna from Paris, Freud left his research position and began a private practice treating primarily emotional disorders.

Freud wrote extensively, and in 1899 published *The Interpretation of Dreams*, which was a first step in the field of psychoanalysis.[52] Freud pioneered new, groundbreaking concepts about the unconscious mind and the repression of unpleasant childhood memories. Instead of hypnosis, however, Freud gave the patient the opportunity to speak freely about any thought entering his or her mind. The goal of this technique was for patients to recognize and thus better deal with repressed emotions that were negatively affecting the person's emotional wellbeing. Later in his career, in the twentieth century, Freud thought the human mind could functionally be conceptualized as having three divisions: id (present from birth, and governing instinctive behavior), ego (which strives to satisfy the id's desires in realistic, socially appropriate ways), and superego (which reflects internalized moral standards that know right from wrong).[53]

There have been many detractors of Sigmund Freud over the years: professionals disagreeing with his concepts of psychoanalysis; others taking issue with his use of cocaine, both professionally and personally, or with his beliefs about woman, which many have interpreted as demeaning. No matter if one agrees with some, most, or none of Freud's concepts, however, no one can deny that Freud introduced a fresh and different way of looking at human behavior. His work was an example of creative human thought based on observation while expounding a coherent conceptual framework.[54]

Women in Medicine in the Nineteenth Century

The nineteenth century was witness to a dramatic change in the perception of women in medicine throughout Western society. It is difficult for us today to understand the extreme prejudice in the past against women becoming physicians. An example of the opinion of the day is reflected in an essay published in the *Boston Medical and Surgical Journal* which stated that, by temperament, women were ill suited for medicine, "Let women not assume the prerogatives of man by entering the arena and noisy business of life, for which she has not the faculties in common with man."[55]

Elizabeth Blackwell (1821–1910), small in stature but strong in courage and intellect, was the first women to challenge this prejudice. Ms. Blackwell was born in Bristol, England, and immigrated with her family to Cincinnati, Ohio, in 1832, motivated by anti-slavery and women rights issues. Elizabeth's professional life began as a schoolteacher, but the death of a friend wishing she had had a female doctor caused Elizabeth to seriously consider the idea of becoming one. She convinced two doctors in Cincinnati to allow her to apprentice with them, as was the custom at that time. Although she was discouraged by most, her neighbor and friend Harriet Beecher Stowe thought it a worthwhile endeavor.

After being rejected by medical schools in New York City, Philadelphia, and elsewhere in the Northeastern USA, Blackwell was accepted to the Geneva Medical College in New York as a practical joke in 1847 (explained in detail in reference 43). Initially shunned by fellow students, she gradually earned the respect of faculty and students on account of her courage and intellect, and graduated first in her class. In 1849, Elizabeth Blackwell was the first woman in the modern world to receive a medical degree. She encountered repeated difficulties finding further training in the U.S., however, and after much rejection she obtained obstetrical training in Paris.[56] Because of an infection she lost sight in one eye, effectively eliminating the possibility of becoming a surgeon; but, still undaunted, she finished her studies. The story of her courage, determination, and talent is well recounted in David McCullough's book, *The Greater Journey: Americans in Paris.*[57] With her younger sister, Dr. Emily Blackwell, and another women physician, Dr. Maria Zakrzewska, Dr. Blackwell founded the New York Infirmary for Women and Children in 1857. This became the first hospital operated by women, in the U.S. and the first to provide clinical training for women.[58] In 1868, Dr. Blackwell founded a Women's Medical College affiliated with her hospital.

Dr. Blackwell returned to England and became a professor of gynecology at the newly formed London School of Medicine for Women in 1875. In her later years she published several books, the most famous being *Pioneer Work in Opening the Medical Profession to Women* in 1895.[59]

Elizabeth Blackwell's admission to medical school and graduation as a medical doctor was a celebrated issue throughout the United States.

Other institutions quickly followed, with the Female Medical College of Pennsylvania, the first medical college for women, opening in 1850 and acquiring a teaching hospital in 1860.[60]

Thereafter Rebecca Lee Crumpler became the first African-American woman to receive an M.D. degree, from the New England Female Medical College, in 1864.[61] The University of Michigan Medical School became the first state school to admit women in 1870. The first Native American woman to receive a medical degree was Susan La Flesche Picotte in 1889.[62] The Johns Hopkins School of Medicine was established in 1893 as a coeducational institution.[63] Dr. Eliza Ann Grier, an emancipated slave, became the first African-American woman licensed for medicine in the state of Georgia.[64] By the end of the nineteenth century, the number of women practicing medicine in the U.S. had increased to 7,000.[65] There can be no doubt that this change in the attitude toward women in medicine that took place in the nineteenth century has dramatically enriched the medical profession.

Summary

The purpose of this brief survey of nineteenth-century medicine was not to be inclusive; it certainly is not. For one thing, none of the people mentioned worked in a vacuum. They had insightful predecessors, colleagues, family, and friends, all of whom had an influence on their work. Many other great accomplishments of the nineteenth century were also not mentioned: Charles Darwin's theory of evolution, the political upheavals that helped shape the twentieth century, and countless other events and discoveries. The purpose of this brief review of many of the major advances in medicine in the nineteenth century was, rather, to share with the reader the awe I have for these people and their accomplishments. They changed our world forever, through human reasoning, keen observation, and clinical and laboratory experimentation producing outstanding insights using the scientific method. Many of these accomplishments flew in the face of long-held misconceptions and superstitions. Some accepted and wanted to be part of the march of medicine; others found it impossible to abandon their cherished, long-held, and in many instances commercially profitable beliefs.

These medical advances of the nineteenth century were not intended for the few, for the wealthy, or for the leaders of society. The heritage of the Enlightenment regarding the importance of all people established the milieu in which physicians and other health-related practitioners found themselves in the nineteenth century, and meant that these scientific advances were meant to benefit all in the society.

With all these advancements in medicine, it remains imperative that we never overlook that medicine will always be an intensely personal experience. Physicians practicing the art of medicine must always use judgment to apply ever-advancing information and capabilities to the individual needs of each patient. For physicians to be able to practice this advanced art of medicine requires a deep personal interest in each and every patient. A trusting relationship that involves the full attention of a physician not distracted by outside influences, such as the present government sanctioned intrusive electronic medical record or time constraints imposed by third-party payers or administrative concerns, is required to achieve excellent results. At the same time, society owes it to every person to have ready access to individualized care. It seems to me that it is in society's interest for every member to be as healthy as possible.

3

THE EARLY YEARS OF AMERICAN MEDICINE AND THE FOUNDING OF THE AMERICAN MEDICAL ASSOCIATION (AMA)

The Early Years of Medicine in the United States

The formal division of the practice of medicine into three distinct categories—physicians, surgeons, and apothecaries—which was in effect in Great Britain in the early-seventeenth century, was not practical in the sparsely populated and poorer new American colonies. So when physicians immigrated to the New World, they had to serve in all three capacities. The first medical book published in the Colonies (in 1677) was entitled *Thatcher's Brief Rule*.[66] The first medical periodical, the *Medical Repository of New York*, began publication in 1797. A regional medical society was formed in New York in 1749. The first statewide medical society was founded in New Jersey in 1766; it still exists today, as the Medical Society of New Jersey, and from its inception has been involved in developing standards for the profession. Other state societies soon followed, in Massachusetts, South Carolina, Delaware, New Hampshire, Connecticut, and Maryland.

Before 1800, unlike the present, there were few university-affiliated medical schools in the newly formed United States, and some experienced many starts and stops.[67] In 1765 Dr. John Morgan founded the first medical school in the United States at the University of Pennsylvania.[68] The second college- or university-affiliated medical school was the Faculty of Physic of King's College in 1767, which in 1891 became Columbia University College of Physicians and Surgeons. Harvard University School of Medicine was founded in 1782[69]; the Geisel School of Medicine at Dartmouth was founded in 1797.[70]

As with other endeavors in this young country, the medical profession was establishing itself with no precedents in place. Early in the nineteenth century, two-thirds of medical practitioners were non-M.D.s, mostly homeopaths (using infinitely small doses of natural substances to treat medical complaints), and a majority of babies were delivered with the assistance of midwives.[71] Physicians and their medical societies thereby found themselves serving as the standard-bearers of an emerging, more scientific, European-style medical tradition by means of establishing regulations, practice standards, and certification standards for physicians—at times sanctioned by the state, at other times not. As medical societies grew, they established their own training programs, which came to be known as "propriety" medical colleges. The Medical Society of the County of New York founded the first of these "propriety" schools in March 1807, and similar schools quickly followed. These schools were successful, in large part, because they did not require preliminary general education, taught little to no basic sciences, had no formal clinical training, and had short time requirements for graduation. It was not until the Flexner Report in 1910, funded by the Carnegie Foundation upon the request of the American Medical Association's Council of Medical Education (itself founded in 1904), that "proprietary" medical schools gradually ceased to exist. The Flexner Report is discussed in detail in Chapter 4.

The model for the first research university medical school with research facilities and an endowment was the Johns Hopkins School of Medicine, founded in 1893. The school had its own hospital, and acknowledged national leaders taught both the science and art of medicine: in medicine, William Osler; in surgery, William Steward Halstead; in pathology, William Henry Welch who also served as dean of the faculty; and in gynecology, Howard Kelley.[72] Clinical practice was required before graduation, and residency programs were introduced.[73] This model is now standard for all physicians training in the U.S.

The Life of Nathan Smith Davis, M.D., A.M., LL.D., founder of the AMA[74]

Nathan Smith Davis, the youngest of seven children, was born on January 9, 1817, on a farm in Chenango County New York. His father, Dow Davis, an orphan, had homesteaded his property and made it suitable for farming. His mother died when Nathan was seven years old. At fifteen, Nathan walked an additional two miles to enhance his learning of English grammar and natural philosophy from a school in an adjoining town. This was in addition to his studies in his own community. His enthusiasm for learning was noticed by the family's physician, Dr. Daniel Clark, who mentioned to Dow Davis that his son Nathan could be a "pill-peddler." Six months later, Dow Davis offered to pay 100 dollars a year to support Nathan so that he could study to become a physician.

Nathan studied English grammar, chemistry, natural philosophy, algebra, and Latin at the Cazenovia Seminary in New York for six months ending in 1834. He then first apprenticed with Dr. Clark, working in exchange for room and board. After a brief period he enrolled in the now-defunct College of Physicians and Surgeons of Western New York in Fairfield, Herkimer County. As was the practice at the time, he was mentored by Dr. Thomas Jackson of Binghamton, New York, and graduated in January 1837. After graduation he practiced for five months in Vienna, New York, where he met and a year later married Anna Marie Parker. At the age of 20 he settled in Binghamton, where he was an active physician for the next ten years. After arriving in Binghamton, Dr. Davis quickly became a leader in the County Medical Society. He wrote many articles for medical journals, with two (in 1840 and 1841) winning essay contests held by the New York State Medical Society. He also taught medical students, extended his studies in Latin and English, edited a local medical journal, and founded and lectured on general topics of interest at the Binghamton Academy.

Dr. Davis became a delegate to the New York Medical Society in 1844, introducing resolutions about medical education and licensure, and he almost immediately was regarded as a central figure in the Society. A major concern of the Society at that time was the large divergence in the training and competence of practicing physicians, considering that this was the dawning of scientific medicine. Noting that one state could not raise standards for the nation, and upon the suggestion of a colleague that a national meeting with state medical societies and medical school representatives could realistically act on raising standards for the profession, Nathan Davis took immediate action. He wrote:

"Whereas, it is believed that a National Convention would be conducive to the elevation of the standard of medical education in the United States; and whereas, there is no mode of accomplishing so desirable an object without concert of action on the part of the medical colleges, societies and institutions of all the states, therefore

"Resolved that the New York State Medical Society earnestly recommends a National Convention of delegates from medical societies and colleges of the whole

*Union, to convene in the City of New York, on the first
Tuesday in May, in the year 1846, for the purpose of
adopting some concerted action on the subject set forth in
the preamble.*

*"Resolved, that a committee of three be appointed to
carry the foregoing resolution into effect."*[75]

Although some delegates thought the resolution impractical because two previous attempts at holding a national convention (in 1835 and 1839) had failed, the resolution passed, and Dr. Davis was appointed to chair the committee of three. The first preliminary national convention indeed took place in New York City in May 1846, when Dr. Nathan Smith Davis was 29 years old. Feeling he needed a bigger platform to more effectively participate in achieving the lofty goals he'd proposed, Dr. Davis left Binghamton and moved his young family to New York City in 1847. He quickly became the Demonstrator of Anatomy at the College of Physicians and Surgeons and Instructor of Medical Jurisprudence. He published a *Text Book of Agriculture* (1848) and after a brief period as assistant editor of the medical journal *The Annalist*, he became the publisher and editor, also in 1848.

On May 5, 1847, with over two hundred delegates from forty medical societies and twenty-eight medical colleges in attendance, Dr. Davis's vision became a reality when the first national medical convention met at the Academy of Natural Sciences in Philadelphia. The enthusiasm there reflected the delegates' intense interest in promoting the values of the profession. Dr. Davis was instrumental in preparing a report arguing for a permanent national medical society to be called the American Medical Association (AMA). Thus, 1847 is recognized as the first official meeting of the AMA. It is of note that the forerunner of the *British Medical Association* was the Provincial and Medical Surgical Association founded in 1832, fifteen years before the first AMA meeting.[76] It was decided in Philadelphia that the delegates to the yearly meeting should come from state, county, and local medical societies and institutions, along with representatives from medical colleges. Thus, on both sides of the Atlantic, the medical profession was undergoing dramatic change and meeting unprecedented challenges because of the spectacular scientific advances occurring in Europe during this century.

Dr. Nathan Davis was present at forty-seven of the first fifty yearly meetings of the AMA. He used all his intellect and persuasive abilities to elevate the standards of medical education and licensure, public health, and clinical and scientific research. He stood for better medical care, against charlatanism, and to have the AMA be the voice of the medical profession in the U.S.A. For example, in 1848, as Chairman of the AMA's Indigenous Medical Botany Committee, he championed the cause of determining the real medicinal value of plant products, vis-à-vis the commercial claims and financial interests of many producers.

In 1849, Dr. Davis became Chair of Physiology and Pathology at Rush Medical College in Chicago. This professorship was added to the medical school faculty to comply with the AMA's recommendations to improve the medical school curriculum. Chicago at that time was a city of about 30,000 lacking city sewer or water facilities, a hospital, or an organization to care for the poor and with no organized medical society. Within a year, in 1850, Davis founded the Illinois General Hospital of the Great Lakes, which exists today as Mercy Hospital, and a state and local medical society. In 1851, at his encouragement, a city sewer system was approved along with a society for care of the poor. He was instrumental in the founding of the Chicago Academy of Sciences; the Chicago Historical Society; the Union College of Law, later to become the Northwestern School of Law; and a home for the treatment of alcoholism.[77] Also in 1851 at the annual AMA meeting, this time in Charleston, S.C., Dr. Davis presented a paper, "An Experimental Inquiry Concerning Some Points Connected with the Process of Assimilation and Nutrition," proving that alcohol lowered body temperature. This concept was so novel, and at the time controversial, that it was not included in the meeting's official publication, the *Transactions*. The paper *was* published in the *Northwestern Medical and Surgical Journal*, of which Davis was an editor.

Davis's book *History of the Medical Profession, from the First Settlement of the British Colonies in America to the Year 1850*, was also published in 1851. Three years later, Dr. Davis was elected Vice-President of the AMA at the convention in St. Louis and presented a resolution regarding, " great sacrifice of health and life which takes place annually, especially among children in large cities, on account of the difficulty of procuring a proper supply of pure and wholesome milk; and the great importance of devising some mode by which the nutritious constituents of the milk can be preserved in their purity and sweetness for such purposes." He then demonstrated powdered milk.[78] This concept, along with Davis's earlier work on the real value of medicinal plants, was the forerunner of several AMA councils and the impetus for passage of our pure food and drug laws. These laws in turn set the stage for the creation of today's Food and Drug Administration (FDA).

It is important to note that today's Food and Drug Administration (FDA) has become a vast bureaucratic maze. The problem seems to be how this agency and the pharmaceutical industry have interacted to create a process resulting in huge costs for the successful development and marketing of new drugs. These costs are hindering the development of much-needed newer antibiotics and other classes of drugs. Somehow this agency and the industry must develop a far less complicated and cheaper development process, while at the same time maintaining safety[79]

In 1855 Dr. Davis published a history of the AMA from its initiation to that year. In 1858, Dr. Davis persuaded the Rush Medical College faculty to adopt many of the recommendations he had championed at the AMA to improve the medical school curriculum. However, the college's Dean, Dr. Daniel Brainard, vetoed the plan. As a result, many of the faculty, including Dr. Davis, left and formed a new medical school, initially the Medical Department of Lind University, which in 1862 became the Chicago Medical College and in 1892 the Northwestern University Medical School. From its inception in 1859, this new medical school followed the majority of the AMA's curricular recommendations, raising entrance requirements and lengthening the course of study to three years. These requirements persuaded the President of Harvard University, William Eliot, to suggest to the faculty of Harvard Medical School that they also adopt these standards, which they did in 1872. Because of its prestige, this action by the Harvard Medical School caused other medical schools in the country to follow suit over the next few decades.

In 1864 the AMA met in New York City and elected its founder, Dr. Nathan Davis, President, which he served for two years. In 1867, Nathan Davis was instrumental in organizing the Association of Medical Colleges, and in 1869 he became President of the Association of Medical Editors. In 1872, Dr. Davis introduced the idea, which was adopted, of creating a Judicial Council. In 1882, that council succeeded in not seating the New York delegation at the yearly meeting for violating the AMA code of ethics by recognizing, "Homoeopaths" (believed *not* to be scientifically based) as members.

Dr. Davis's life was not without its share of tragedy, as he and his wife, Anna, suffered through the untimely death in 1880 of their oldest son, Dr. Frank Howard Davis, secondary to a bacterial infection that would be easily treated today. In 1882, both their daughter and *her* daughter died, and a year later their daughter's husband died, leaving six orphaned children who moved in with and were raised by their grandparents.[80] It is difficult for us living today to recognize the pain that so many families had to endure because of frequent untimely deaths even in the nineteenth and early twentieth centuries.

In 1882, Dr. Davis spoke in support of a resolution for the publication of a weekly medical journal to replace the yearly *Transactions* and the necessary changes to the Constitution to effect this change. Dr. Davis felt the need for further research on specific problems and for the dissemination of knowledge on the results of that research. He also wanted a forum for collegial interaction among members that a weekly journal could provide. In 1883 at the yearly convention in Cleveland, Dr. Davis, holding the position of Chairman of the Board of Directors, reported that 2,100 pledges to sustain a weekly AMA journal had been received. This, he reported, would ensure the financial viability of the project. A printing company in Chicago with the lowest bid was selected; Dr. Davis then resigned as a Trustee and was endorsed by the convention to be the first editor-in-chief of the new journal, and the American Association of Medical Editors also endorsed him for that position on June 5, 1883, at *its* convention. (Dr. Davis was also President of *that* organization.) Later that year, Dr. Davis, now 65, became the first editor of the *Journal of the American Medical Association;* Vol. 1, No. 1, was published on July 14, 1883. The Journal had remarkable success and was already recognized as one of the nation's leading medical journals by the time Dr. Davis resigned as editor in 1888.

At the founding of the *Journal*, the Board, wishing to appear beyond reproach, asked the editor to be prudent regarding advertising in the new journal. "He was asked to solicit advertisements from all medical educational institutions and hospitals open for clinical instruction, from book publishers, pharmaceutical companies, instrument makers, and all other legitimate business interests. But all advertisements of *propriety, trademark,* copyrighted or patented medicines should be excluded. Neither should any advertisements be admitted with one or more names of members of the profession as indorsers, having their *official titles* or *positions* attached. In other words, no advertisements should be admitted which fairly contravene in letter or spirit the principles of the national code of ethics."[81]

Lofty directives from the Board of Directors are one thing; financing a new journal in order to keep it financially self-supporting may prove to be an entirely different matter. A published letter from a physician in Burlington, Iowa, reflects on the reality of that time: "*Dear Doctor:* I have received your first number and am delighted with it as a journal; but I am not so pleased with your advertisements. Parke, Davis & Co. has bored the physicians of the Northwest sufficiently with their ready-made prescriptions. In fact, they have taken the place of Ayer's Pectoral and Humbold's Buchu and are patronized by all quacks and all the patent medicine men in this country. Soon I presume you will advertise Warner's safe cure for kidney trouble. Now, I protest right here against the organ of the American Medical Association being the means of disseminating any such advertisements. I ask a place for this in your correspondence column, and see if I am not endorsed by nine tenths of the physicians in the land."[82]

The founding of the weekly *AMA Journal* carried with it certain associations that we now would look upon as controversial. Advertising revenue was critical in order to maintain the financial viability of the journal. Consequently, income from cigarette and pharmaceutical companies helped sustain the publication, even though the safety or scientific validity of these products was certainly open to question.

Today, many are leery of the degree that medical publications and meetings are dependent on advertising from various sources, despite the claims of complete independence. The problem is that many of the same people doing the complaining are also not willing to pay the significantly higher prices required for a commercial-free experience.

While editing the AMA Journal, Nathan Davis in 1884 published another book, *Principles and Practice of Medicine* that was so successful that a second edition was published in 1886. The second edition was a forerunner by six years of Dr. William Olser's most influential text, *The Principles and Practice of Medicine: Designed for the Use of Practitioners and Students of Medicine.* This latter book is credited with the beginning of philanthropic giving, making possible the development of an

American version of the great scientific leaps in medicine taking place in Europe. Dr. Osler, like many of his colleagues who were the acknowledged leaders in academic medicine, was active in the young AMA. This sort of relationship, however, is less so today.

At the 1884 AMA yearly meeting, it was decided to invite the International Medical Congress to meet in Washington, D.C., in 1887. So much acrimony developed as to who would be on the committee arranging the meeting, however, that cancellation was possible. All was settled, though, when in 1885, Dr. Austin Flint, a brilliant cardiac diagnostician who in 1862 had explained the physiology of the apparent heart murmur of mitral valve stenosis in the presence of aortic valve insufficiency,[83] was made President and Dr. Davis Secretary-General of the Congress. When Dr. Flint unexpectedly died of a stroke in 1886, Dr. Davis assumed the presidency, later traveling to Great Britain to invite members of the British Medical Society to the Congress. The Congress was a resounding success, with Dr. Davis receiving worldwide recognition.

Dr. Davis became an Emeritus Professor at Northwestern University School of Medicine in 1892, although he continued to teach medical history through 1897. Then, after having served as Dean of the medical school and its predecessors for thirty-five years, he became Dean Emeritus of Northwestern University Medical School in 1898.

The AMA at 50

In 1897, the AMA celebrated its fiftieth anniversary, holding its annual meeting at the site of its official founding in Philadelphia. Its founder, Dr. Nathan Smith Davis was now eighty years old. The AMA had become somewhat successful and exercised some limited national influence, owing mostly to the publication of the *Journal of the American Medical Association (JAMA)*. At this meeting, Dr. Davis delivered a speech he titled "A Brief History of the Origin of the American Medical Association, the Principles on Which it Was Organized, the Object it Was Designated to Accomplish, and How Far they had Been Attained During the Half Century of its Existence."[84] In 1903, Dr. Davis published his last book, *History of Medicine*. The following year he died of a heart attack at the age of eighty-seven.

The early success of the AMA was, I believe, the result of several factors. Foremost was the fact that as reviewed in Chapters 1 & 2, the advancements derived from applying science in medicine resulted in great benefits for mankind. Medicine went from an itinerant industry based on superstition to a learned profession that attracted incredibly talented women and men. These physicians understood the need to formalize the education of future physicians, the importance of physicians' promoting public health, the critical impact of good hospitals, and the need to base their treatments as much as possible on scientific evidence. At the same time, they understood the need to individualize each patient's needs, and to adapt the relevant scientific knowledge to the specific situation of each patient: the special relationship between physician and patient was recognized to be paramount with regard to the success of the profession. And because of the democratization of the AMA, each member felt part of the decision-making process, fostering a collegial atmosphere along with widespread acceptance of the goals and direction of the organization.

The question for the AMA, as with many successful organizations, is will the Association be able to stay true to its founding values, or will it be seduced by wealth and power?

Medical Ethics

At the preliminary National Medical Convention in 1846, a resolution on medical ethics was put forward that remains influential today. "[I]t is expedient," the resolution affirmed, "that the medical profession in the United States should be governed by the same code of medical ethics, and that a committee of seven be appointed to report a code for that purpose at a meeting to be held in Philadelphia on the first Wednesday of May 1847."[85] That committee presented its report in 1847, giving full credit to the work on medical ethics of Dr. Thomas Percival, a Fellow of the Royal Society of England. Dr. Percival had submitted the first code of medical ethics to the English medical profession early in the 1790's; he published a revised copy in 1803 after consultation with many notables, including Charles White, William Heberdon, John Hunter, William Withering, and Erasmus Darwin.

The New York Medical Society was the first in the U.S. to adopt the Percival code of medical ethics in 1823, followed by the Baltimore

Medical Society in 1832. Although it has been modified over the years, the basic principles are timeless: service to the individual patient—that was and is the core value of medicine—"professional behavior," improvements in public health and sanitation, lifelong learning, advancement of the science of medicine, exposure of quackery, and service in the best interests of the nation.[86] "Medicine has for years depended for its success on the personal relationship between physician and patient. Every article in the principle of ethics is designed to emphasize this relationship."[87]

This relationship has to be personal for it to be truly therapeutic. The present ten-minute visits with the physician equally involved with a computer keyboard rather than in giving 100 percent attention to the patient will not suffice. That is why for any medical system to be both beneficial and efficient, the patient-doctor relationship must be strengthened and not compromised. A hospital cannot be your doctor; an insurance company cannot be your doctor; a government cannot be your doctor. Only you and a knowledgeable, empathetic, caring physician with adequate time can establish a successful health care relationship.

In my opinion, the best way to achieve this is for all Americans through tax policy to be able to fund and thus be completely in charge of their every day care. Insurance, as it was initially intended, should be reserved for high-ticket items. This model requires price transparency, and market forces—to determine the value of physician and hospital services rather than the present failed price-fixed system.[88]

4
The Struggle of Regulars to Control Medical Practice through Licensure

 By the 1830s, several states had passed laws authorizing state medical societies formed by Regulars, those believing in science and formal
training in medicine, to issue licenses to whomever they felt appropriate. These laws had little meaning, however, as there were no specified
criteria and no penalties for practicing medicine without such a license.
In some states, licensed physicians could sue for collection of their fees,
but the courts rarely upheld these suits.

The two recognized professions in early America were lawyers, who
were sanctioned and policed by the courts, and military officers, who
were promoted (and court-martialed) by fellow officers. Both received
remuneration for their efforts without regard to the eventual outcome
of their work. Clergy were considered something like a profession, with
the authority to administer legally binding marriages, but they were not
policed or sanctioned by the authority of the state. With the founding
of the American Medical Association in 1847 came the realization that
they, the Regulars, the purveyors of scientific medicine, wanted to have
exclusive state-sanctioned recognition as professionals, like lawyers and
military officers.

Medicine would not be recognized as a profession, however, until
1889. In that year, the U. S. Supreme Court upheld a West Virginia law
that provided for a medical board backed by the power of the state to
fine and imprison anyone practicing medicine without a license.[89]

Six years after its establishment, the American Medical Association
continued to propound strong views on professionalism and licensure.
In his presidential address at the annual meeting in 1853, Dr. Beverly R.
Wellford spoke in favor of having legislation passed in every state creating a board of medical examiners to evaluate and certify all wishing to
care for the sick. It was understood that the criteria used would be those
sanctioned by the AMA. Sixteen years later, the AMA, having met with
little success regarding licensure, passed the following resolution at its
yearly meeting in 1869: "That each state medical society be requested
to require its examining board or boards to exact of every applicant for

examination adequate proof that he has a proper general education, is twenty-one years of age, and has pursued the study of medicine three full years, one year of which time shall have been at a regularly organized medical college, whose curriculum embraces adequate facilities for didactic, demonstrative, and hospital clinical instruction."[90] By today's standards this was inadequate, allowing for two years of apprenticeship and only one year of formal medical school training, but at that time it was quite forward thinking and demanding. The apparent resistance of state legislators to enact strict licensing laws derived from the inability of scientific medicine, at that time, to demonstrate superior outcomes for non-surgical problems.

Dr. James Reeves, the Medical Society of West Virginia, Licensure, and the U.S. Supreme Court [91]

At first glance, Dr. James Reeves appeared to be similar to the many poorly trained, mid-nineteenth-century medical practitioners common throughout rural America at that time. In reality however, he was an extremely bright, forward-thinking physician: He was a fervent believer in the scientific basis of medicine and an active member of the AMA. Despite having little formal medical training, Dr. Reeves, while practicing medicine in his hometown of Philippi, West Virginia, in 1851 successfully contained a typhoid fever epidemic.* In 1859 he published a treatise on typhoid fever, which quickly became a standard text in the most prestigious medical schools in America. Hungry for more formal medical training, Dr. Reeves left Philippi in 1859 and entered the University of Pennsylvania School Of Medicine; he graduated with a medical degree in 1860. During his lifetime he published twenty-two medical articles, four medical textbooks, and a handbook on medical microscopy.[92]

> * Typhoid fever is caused by the bacteria *Salmonella enterica serotype typhi* and is spread by the fecal-oral route. A vaccine is available, but it is not 100% effective. Other related bacteria can cause similar illnesses. Chronic carriage is possible and is a means of infecting many others. The disease typically presents early with fevers, then later manifests as abdominal pain and possible skin lesions. This is followed by diarrhea or possibly constipation and intestinal bleeding. If untreated, typhoid fever can cause death. Today it can be treated if necessary with modern antibiotics, but resistant organisms are becoming more prevalent.

Just after the carnage of the Civil War and four years after the creation of West Virginia as a separate state (having been carved out from Virginia after its secession), Dr. Reeves, by this time a recognized medical leader, founded the Medical Society of West Virginia (MSWV) in 1867. West Virginia being a new state, many organizations that had existed in other states needed to be created de novo, thus creating an atmosphere of greater political flexibility. Demonstrating his political acumen and ability to convince other medical leaders in the state of the importance of scientific medicine, Reeves held the first meeting of his new state society in April 1867. This allowed the Society to send representatives to the AMA's national meeting in May. The twenty-one other Regulars joining Reeves met in the West Virginia State Capitol building in the Senate Chambers. The politically well-connected B&O Railroad provided free transportation to those Regulars wishing to attend. Reeves's inaugural address, almost religious in nature, stated that the future of medicine and the health of the nation depended on the practice of scientifically based medicine by well-trained practitioners graduating from reputable medical schools. He was in effect endorsing himself, and castigating those who believed in different philosophies of medicine or who did not graduate from medical schools that taught scientific medicine. Some Regulars who were more tolerant of those practicing other disciplines* were criticized by this new group of Regulars making up the MSWV, who were intent on prohibiting others from practicing medicine.

* E.g. homeopaths, botanics, eclectics, Thomsonians, hydropaths, and rural healers with home remedies were all practicing medicine for a fee.

In 1872, the incoming President of the MSWV, Dr. James Lazzelle, proposed legal action to protect the public from the dangers of treatments by non-Regulars. He advocated a licensing law to be passed by the West Virginia state legislature ensuring that only qualified practitioners, as determined by the MSWV, could practice in the state under penalty of law. Dr. Lazzelle's proposals met with mixed reviews. Many supported a law that provided for strict state-mandated penalties for anyone other than AMA-eligible physicians practicing medicine. Others were concerned, however, that the legislature would pass a law so broad that just about any practitioner would be licensed.

In 1874, incoming MSWV president Dr. Silas W. Hall asserted that a strong licensing law was needed, but his efforts at the legislature were greeted with apathy and denial. Hall's successor, Dr. Mathew Campbell, who was more politically savvy, worked to convince the doubting members of the legislature of the feasibility of strong licensing laws and established alliances with Democratic political leaders. By 1876, most physicians had joined with many West Virginians who had left the Republican Party because of their opposition to Reconstruction, thereby aligning themselves with the political powers in the state. Outgoing Democratic governor John J. Jacob was invited by Campbell to be the first non-physician to address the yearly meeting of the MSWV. Governor Jacob thereupon proposed that the citizens of the state would benefit, in terms of public health and medical practice, from the practice of scientific medicine upheld by the MSWV.

Reeves and his colleagues at the MSWV wanted a strong licensing law, but knew that it would take cunning, planning, and patience to make it happen. In 1877, the first, seemly innocuous step was a proposal that the legislature create a state Board of Health, which as of 1876 already existed in seven other states.*[93] This idea followed an AMA initiative at its national meeting in 1875 endorsing the concept of a State Board of Health for every state in the union. Following this endorsement, the then President of the AMA sent letters to the governors of states that did not have a State Board of Health endorsing the idea. The seed was thereby planted that every forward-looking state would have a Board of Health. Reeves' second step was to appoint Dr. George Baird, former mayor of Wheeling† and an ardent proponent of scientifically based medicine, to head the newly created standing committee on legislation that would coordinate lobbying efforts. Baird had recently succeeded Reeves as Wheeling's health officer, in which position both had been strong advocates of clean water and efficient waste treatment.

* Alabama, California, Massachusetts, Michigan, Minnesota, Virginia, and Wisconsin.

† An industrialist and leader in the state secession movement who was extremely well connected politically.

Many in the MSWV were not as doctrinaire about enforcing strict AMA guidelines, as were Reeves and Baird. Their leader was Dr. William Dent, who was from a well-established West Virginia medical family in the central part of the state, and was elected President of the MSWV in 1879. Dent wanted the MSWV to be more lenient in its attitude toward non-Regulars, an issue that at the time had divided the

New York Medical Society. The Dent family was, as we will see, to provide the legal challenge to the Reeves and Baird plan that eventually was resolved by a U.S. Supreme Court decision in 1889. To thwart Dent, the next year, in 1880, Reeves and Baird regained control of the society by successfully electing Dr. William Van Kirk, an ardent follower of theirs, as President. They then planned an all-out effort to pass a Board of Health law at the 1881 biennial session of the West Virginia legislature. Reeves assumed the leadership position for this lobbying effort; and with Baird's political acumen, the society helped elect six of its members, five to the House and one to the Senate, to the 1881 legislative session. Reeves meanwhile enlisted the help of James H. Ferguson, lead attorney for the C&O railroad, as legal and political advisor. Ferguson was also running for, and was elected to, the state House of Representatives.

With advice from others, Reeves crafted the bill he wanted passed into law. He resurrected the concept of creating a Board of Health for the safety and welfare of the people of the state; at the end of the bill he added a small section that authorized this board to also oversee licensing of the practice of medicine with state-backed police powers. As both he and Baird had established themselves as leaders in public health both locally and in national societies, and as other states were also establishing boards of public health, his bill on the surface seemed quite reasonable, with medical licensure appearing as a minor provision. Reeves' goal, however, was to eventually limit medical practice to Regulars who had earned M.D. degrees from reputable, scientifically rigorous schools, and he wanted this Board of Health to have the authority of the state to punish those practicing without these credentials. The governor would appoint the Board of Health with these powers with members by law limited to Regulars, who had graduated from appropriate medical schools and had been in practice for at least twelve years.

Reeves' bill proposed three routes to obtaining a certificate to practice medicine—not at that time called a license, a word he thought might raise the ire of some legislators. The first pathway was graduation from an acceptable medical school as defined by the board, an acceptable school being one that that followed AMA guidelines as to curriculum. The second path was to pass a test, administered by two members of the state board, covering the AMA Regular medical school curriculum—the method of examination to be determined by the board. The third route to certification, meant to minimize objections from established practitioners, was proof of continuous practice in West Virginia for at least ten years before passage of the law. The penalties for practicing any form of medicine without a certificate would be harsh and for the first time in this country would involve the imposition of fines and/or imprisonment under state law. With James Ferguson leading the way in the legislature, the support of both the C&O and B&O railroads, and Reeves emphasizing the public health aspects of the law both to the press and to leaders of the House and Senate, and after much wrangling in both chambers, Reeves' bill was passed with minor revisions and signed into law by the newly elected governor, Jacob B. Jackson, on March 8, 1881.

The governor thereupon immediately appointed the new board, two for six-year terms and four for four-year terms. Reeves, one of the six-year members, became Secretary and head of the Board, and he believed he needed to quickly demonstrate the effectiveness of the new law, especially because doubters would be poised to attack it at the next year's special legislative session. An epidemic of smallpox* that summer in Pittsburg gave Reeves reason to immediately spring into action, as he had acted to control the typhoid epidemic in 1851. He ordered all shipping from Pennsylvania to be quarantined, and also ordered inspection of all overland travelers from that area. Having demonstrated the salutary public health benefits of a Board of Health, Reeves then turned his attention to licensing West Virginia's physicians. He sent forms to every physician in the state seeking proof of practice for ten years or proof of a medical degree, or else requiring an application for examination. The Board was then kept busy approving most applications and denying a few. Reeves easily overcame various attempts to undermine it in ensuing legislative sessions. In 1882 he was elected by delegates at the AMA national meeting to its National Judiciary Council. They recognized the breakthrough that Reeves had obtained by having his state in essence enforce AMA criteria to practice medicine, and no doubt hoped to implement the West Virginia model throughout the country. More hurdles had to be overcome, however, before that would happen.

* A viral disease that before vaccination was deadly, as described in Chapter 2.

The greatest challenges to the Board came from none other than the Dent family. The family of Dr. William Dent, past president of the MSWV who had done his best, but failed, to dethrone Reeves and Baird, provided the legal test cases challenging the Board of Health.

The first challenge came from Arthur Dent, William Dent's nephew who failed an oral examination, apparently on technicalities, on January 13, 1882. Arthur then spent a month at a medical school in Ohio, received an M.D. degree (over the disapproval of at least one faculty member), and returned to the Board with degree in hand, demanding a certificate (license) to practice. In order to refuse Arthur's second attempt, the Board had to define for the first time the meaning of a reputable medical school. They in essence followed the previously published AMA guidelines making reference to the curriculum of the established major medical schools. Arthur was as a result denied a certificate, whereupon he moved to another state.

William Dent himself had previously been awarded a certificate based on his years in practice, but his son, Frank M. Dent, presented a more complex situation. There was confusion as to a certificate that was assumed to be granted to William's father, Marmaduke Dent, that William wished to be for his son. Frank foolishly practiced for a period under cover of a confused certificate; then, unable to qualify under the ten-year rule and after exploring other options, enrolled in an Eclectic medical school* and within weeks received a degree. He then sought a certificate on the basis of that degree, but was denied one by the Board and threatened with legal action if he continued to practice. The Dents decided that Frank should continue to practice, thereby forcing the Board to apply its legal penalties, and then appealed through the court system for relief from Reeves' law, in essence trying to overturn the law via the courts.

* An Eclectic medical college opened in Cincinnati in 1844, teaching the virtues of using natural derivatives for cures, as opposed to the teachings of the Greeks and Romans frequently referred to at that time. [94]

The Dents entrusted their legal attack on the law to Frank's cousin and Arthur Dent's younger brother, Marmaduke Dent, an extremely bright, aggressive, and well-respected lawyer. The initial trial took place in Circuit Court in April 1883. Frank had pleaded not guilty, but the Grand Jury found reason for trial and the Circuit Court found Frank guilty of practicing without a license and fined him $50.00. Marmaduke immediately appealed Frank's conviction to the State Supreme Court, where Marmaduke could appeal the merits of the Board's actions on constitutional grounds.

Marmaduke's constitutional argument was based on the Fourteenth

Amendment to the U.S. Constitution, passed in 1868. This amendment was a response to the various laws passed by Southern states after their defeat in the Civil War limiting the constitutional rights of the newly freed slaves. It states, "No State shall make or enforce any law which shall abridge the privileges or immunities of citizens of the United States; nor shall any State deprive any person of life, liberty, or property, without due process of law; nor deny to any person within its jurisdiction the equal protection of the laws."[95] Among many other points, Marmaduke also argued that the Board of Health law was misguided because it compelled one approach to the practice of medicine, arbitrarily excluding all others.* The Attorney General of the state, Cornelius Clarkson Watts, countered that under the Tenth Amendment to the Constitution, states had all powers not specifically assigned to the federal government, and that public health was a proper state concern. He noted that other states had passed laws regarding surgery and the dispensing of dangerous drugs.

* To the disdain of the practitioners of other concepts of medicine, some Regulars were still practicing based on the old Greek and Roman concepts of balancing the life forces of blood, black bile, yellow bile, and phlegm. By this time however, most Regulars had abandoned these concepts in favor of the medical science being discovered in the nineteenth century, as described in Chapter 2.

The West Virginia Supreme Court heard the case on June 17, 1884, and rendered a unanimous opinion in favor of the Board of Health law on November 1. The court's opinion was based on several points. Although some of the justices had sympathy for Marmaduke's contention that the Board of Health law was poor public policy, the court decided that the law could be nullified only if it violated specific constitutional provisions. State legislators, it noted, had legitimate police powers to regulate business and occupational interests so as to benefit the public welfare: States required lawyers to be licensed, for example, to protect the public, and the same should hold true with respect to physicians. Courts could not strike down laws, it ruled, because they believed they were not the best possible solution to a problem; they could do so only if a law violated a constitutional principle.

It was not long before the AMA and Regulars in other states hailed the West Virginia Supreme Court's decision and called for similar laws in their states. The Dents felt that justice was not served, however, and they appealed to the U.S. Supreme Court. Meanwhile, Reeves and his board vigorously enforced their position that medicine was a learned profession with practitioners needing to earn an advanced degree from schools with a strong scientific curriculum in accordance with strict AMA standards.

The Supreme Court heard the case on December 11, 1888. Marmaduke argued that the Board of Health was removing a property right (to earn a living) from Frank Dent without due process. The requirement that an applicant obtain a certificate (in reality a license) via an exam administered and judged by the same board, he argued, was arbitrary and capricious; the Court could set an example of the power of the Fourteenth Amendment by finding in favor of his client.

Defending the state was the new state Attorney General, Alfred Caldwell, Jr., who invoked the states' police powers under the Tenth Amendment rights, especially to prevent harm to the general welfare and on the basis that quality medical and health care were surely in the public interest. He noted that other states had passed laws restricting property rights in order to protect public health; due process requirements were not absolute, he maintained, especially in areas pertaining to public health. The West Virginia law should be upheld, he argued, as it was intended to elevate the practice of medicine in the state; the state board was following AMA guidelines with regard to ethics and its high standards for medical education, established by the best medical minds in the country. Furthermore, he contended, because Frank Dent had not submitted to an exam by the Board of Health, he could not claim that the board was acting in a capricious manner.

The Supreme Court rendered its unanimous decision on January 14, 1889, in favor of West Virginia's Board of Health law. The Court's stated reasons were many. Citizens have the right, it noted, to pursue any lawful activity, subject to restrictions applied to all; medicine requires extensive and special skills, and like the law is a profession. The West Virginia law was not administered as punishment for previous actions, but was intended to protect the public in the future. Moreover, states have a special interest in protecting the general welfare, and are free to make their own decisions with respect to what is best policy to protect their citizens' public health. In addition, "due process" is a vague term, and its proper implementation must be evaluated on an individual basis.

Following this Supreme Court ruling, James Reeves and his colleagues at the MSWV could now proceed on the assumption that their ability to license physicians, in accordance with AMA guidelines, would determine the practice of medicine in the United States from 1889 onward. But it is worth noting that their justification for these licensing laws and limiting the practice of medicine to the "Regulars" would have been nonexistent without the tremendous progress in medical science that had taken place during the nineteenth century, as briefly described in Chapter 2. Vaccination was for the first time in human history beginning to combat many devastating contagious diseases. Bacterial diseases were being understood, and the pathological bases of organ dysfunction were being described. Anesthesia was enabling the advancement of surgery. These developments held real promise for future cures. And who would best be able to translate future scientific advances into clinical therapies than scientifically well-trained physicians?

The scientific method that developed in the late Renaissance, as it was briefly described in Chapter 1, was rapidly increasing man's knowledge, and that knowledge was destined to increase at an ever-accelerating pace. But this paradigm of ever-increasing scientific knowledge in medicine would demand that the AMA, and the Regulars, ensure that the nation's medical schools had rigorous and demanding scientific curricula. What would prove much more difficult would be how to assure physicians' ability to practice scientific, compassionate, and rational medicine throughout their careers—not just their capabilities as they began their practice.

The Evolution of Medical Licensure in the United States

Ahead of its time, in 1897 at the annual AMA meeting, the Medical Society of California proposed a National Board of Medical Examiners to provide for uniform testing to obtain a medical license. The national convention rejected this suggestion[96]; but the states, as the practice of medical licensure spread throughout the nation, continued to develop and administer their own criteria and tests. It soon became apparent, however, that each state creating its own assessment of medical knowledge was confusing and redundant. In an attempt to coordinate state licensing responsibilities, the Federation of State Medical Boards was founded in 1912. Then, in 1915, the National Board of Medical Examiners (NBME) was founded to create a uniform, national, high-quality written examination covering the many aspects of medical knowledge.[97] It took another thirty years, however, until after World War II, for states to start relying more on national exams rather than their own.[98]

To verify the credentials of foreign medical school graduates entering the United States to obtain our more advanced post-graduate training, the Educational Commission for Foreign Medical Graduates (ECFMG) was established in 1956. In 1992, the NBME, in conjunction with the Federation of State Medical Boards and the ECFMG, utilized the United States Medical Licensing Examination (USMLE), which is now the standard written assessment test in medicine.[99] The American Medical Association was present at the founding of all these credentialing entities and has board representation on all of them.

The USMLE test consists of three distinctly separate sections, each about eight hours long. The first part is intended to test the applicant's mastery of the basic sciences related to medicine. The second section tests the applicant's mastery of the scientific bases of clinical medicine, and the third consists of a more practical clinical assessment. For those attending American medical schools, Part I is usually taken after the second year, Part II during the fourth year, and Part III during the first post-graduate year. Foreign medical school graduates must take and pass the three tests before entering any residency program in the United States.* To be licensed in any state in the U.S., an applicant must receive a passing grade on all three USMLE tests. In addition, the state must receive a medical school transcript, documentation of having successfully graduated from an accredited post–medical school residency, and explanation of hospital disciplinary action, if any, before a license is issued. In case one needs to make application to various states during one's career, the Federation Credentials Verification Service (FCVS) was founded in 1996 to store and verify these credentials in case they were needed in the future.

> * Even though I took these tests over forty years ago, I still remember studying for and taking each one of them.

Every residency program must also undergo its own accreditation process, conducted by the Accreditation Council for Graduate Medical Education (ACGME). The ACGME was founded in 1981 by the American Board of Medical Specialties, the American Hospital Association, the American Medical Association, the Association of Medical Colleges, and the Council of Medical Specialty Societies. Each one of these vast arrays of licensing and credentialing entities has its own staff and officers and requires funding at various levels. Thus what started out in

1889 as a licensing law with the rationale of protecting the public has morphed into a very large and expensive industry, with little to no attempt made at consolidation so as to decrease the bureaucratic burden and save resources. Certainly an attempt to streamline these organizations, with careful studies evaluating the effectiveness of any changes, would be welcome.

The Problem of Assessing Continued Competence *after* Issuance of Licensure

For many decades in all states, once a medical license was issued, it was valid indefinitely after certain required criteria were met, including that the physician had remained free of criminal charges, that periodic fees were paid to the state licensing board, and that a prescribed number of hours of continuing medical education (CME) were completed: usually about 150 hours over three years, or about 50 hours each year. Licenses would rarely be forfeited. Since 2000, the American Board of Medical Specialties (ABMS) has been working on a process it felt was necessary to demonstrate to the public and to interested third parties that periodic testing and documentation are necessary above and beyond the CME process. The Board has called this Maintenance of Certification (MOC).

This additional testing would at the same time greatly increase the various boards' revenue streams, leading many to question its motives. Although cloaked in a concern for the need for physicians to deliver up-to-the-minute high-quality care, the reason government and other third-party payers are concerned for this additional need of assessment is mostly to address our nations "unsustainable cost increases."[100] However, given Medicare price-fixing, a lack of industry wide price transparency, and patients and their physicians removed from cost responsibility, it appears that physicians under these conditions would be unable to effectively participate in cost control despite MOC.[101]

When instituting the MOC process, the ABMS, fearing legal repercussions, excluded from needing recertification those physicians who had been certified before 1990, because at that time they were certified for life. The appeal of this program has been questioned, because only 1 percent of those not required to recertify have done so.[102] The emerging evidence is that MOC does NOT improve patient care.[103] As a means of forcing physicians to participate in MOC, the ABMS has successfully lobbied Congress to impose Medicare payment penalties on those not recertified, an example of "regulatory capture."[104] Physicians are now caught in a financial bind, paying for an unpopular testing process that is of questionable value or earning less from the country's largest third-party payer.*

> * Quite ironic as the third party system rather than patient directed care is responsible for the escalating costs.

The design of MOC is based on the six domains developed the by the ABMS and the ACGME; they at this time constitute the bible for medical education, although to many they appear arbitrary and without direct evidence of benefit. They are: medical knowledge, patient care and procedural skills, interpersonal and communication skills, professionalism, practice-based learning and improvement, and systems-based practice (the setting in which one practices). A more direct and simpler set of goals for medical education, in my view, would be developed if we had a patient-centered and not a third-party-centered health care system. In a patient-centered system, patients use their own money from health savings accounts to pay physicians. In that situation, for physicians to be successful they would have to demonstrate caring for the welfare of their patients and communicate with them in clear and concise language. Physicians would need to understand the benefits and limits of present-day medical science and treatments, and to know evidence-based medicine and be able to tailor it to individual patients' specific needs.

Currently, in our government-centered, heavily regulated system, MOC has four criteria for recertification: possession of a valid medical license; adequate participation in continuing medical education; cognitive expertise, as demonstrated by extensive testing similar to USMLE Parts I, II, and III, at intervals prescribed by the specific board (usually every ten years); and satisfactory evaluation of the quality of care offered by comparison with peers and national standards and with assessments of improvement. The first two were standard before 1990; the second two are new and felt by many physicians to be onerous and excessive. The ABMS is attempting to have the continuance of a medical license in all states dependent on all four of its criteria being met; state medical societies in Ohio, Michigan, and New York have passed resolutions against continuance of licensure being dependent on successfully completing MOC and have so far been successful. The ABMS is also seeking support from hospitals to enforce its criteria with regard to maintaining staff privileges, and this also is a major issue for state medical societies.

It appears the ABMS is continuing on the same path followed in past decades by organized medicine and by the ever-increasing alphabet soup of credentialing entities: that of seeking support, mostly from third-party payers, for adding on more complex knowledge-based testing. But medical mishaps are not the result of lack of knowledge, which is readily available on any computer or smart phone. The best way to improve patient care and avoid mistakes is for physicians to readily discuss their patients with each other and listen to others' ideas and recommendations.[105] Accordingly, we need a continuous process that enhances communication skills by emphasizing physician interaction, with discussion of cases around difficult issues. This certainly can be accomplished within the present CME system, perhaps enhanced with computer-generated post-tests. Opposition to maintenance of certification and to the American Board of Internal Medicine and the ABMS is gaining momentum to the point of the creation by practicing physicians of a new certifying body, the National Board of Physicians and Surgeons.[106] Why is the pushback from practicing physicians so forceful other than the obvious fraud, as mentioned in reference 106? It turns out MOC testing is irrelevant. All practicing internists and other physicians do NOT practice in the entire specialty that is the basis for MOC testing. Most of their practice involves a limited number of diagnoses. Thus each physician has an individual need for specific information and usually tailors their learning to meet those unique needs. To most physicians MOC is onerous, expensive, time consuming and irrelevant.

Licensing the Scope of Practice of Non-Physician Health Personnel

The issue of expanding the scope of practice without physician supervision for advanced practice nurses (NP) and physician assistants (PA) by modifying their licensing has recently been reignited. This issue has become intensified, as many believe there will be a physician shortage because of the aging of the population and the need for increased access to health care. This perception of shortage may or may not be real, however, especially if patients had more freedom to choose their physicians utilizing optimized universal tax-credited health savings accounts

(HSAs), explained further in chapter 10, with the option of direct care contracts.[107] These contracts differ from the older concept of concierge medicine by being much more affordable. Costs range from about $30/month to about $150/month depending on location, family size, and practice model. These practices usually arrange for testing and drugs at far reduced rates. An unintended consequence of the large deductibles in many of the policies under the Affordable Care Act is the dramatic increase in popularity of these contracts.[108] [109]

As approximately 80 percent of health care is consumed by 20 percent of the population—those with chronic diseases[110]—and with direct care contracts giving more choice, their primary care could be provided by Internal Medicine sub-specialists or Neurologists depending on the chronic condition. If this were to occur, market forces would then reveal whether or not there really is a doctor shortage.

Direct care contracts take place when a patient pays a physician a monthly fee to provide care. Ideally, with changes in federal law this fee could be paid from a health savings account.

Would licensing of NPs and PAs for outpatient care of relatively simple matters without physician supervision significantly impact the delivery of primary care, possibly? I suggest limiting their licensing to nonprocedural care of those who are not chronically ill, and whose complaints are minor and immediate. With the widespread use of direct care contracts, however, primary care physicians would probably be more available to meet the nation's primary care needs. Competition would exist, and the market would determine the result.

5

Major AMA Accomplishments in the Early Twentieth Century

An excerpt from an editorial in *JAMA* (the *Journal of the American Medical Association*) published early in 1901 reflects the underlying philosophy of the organization and its recognition of the profound changes caused by the introduction of science into the practice of medicine. At that point in time, the AMA was on the right side of history. "The medical college in the coming century will have to give more attention to the quality of its output, if present signs are not misleading. Human nature will not change; there will be deceivers and their followers, but this will only accentuate the demand for higher qualifications in our profession. The future of science is not in doubt; the world will not stop in its progress nor lose what it has gained, *but the future of the medical profession is in its own hands and can only be assured by its living up to its highest ideals.*"[111] (Italics added.)

AMA Reorganization, 1901

Although the publication of the *Journal of the American Medical Association*, beginning in 1883, did enhance the prestige of the organization, most scientifically oriented physicians, "Regulars," were still not members. In 1900 there were about 100,000 Regular physicians in the U.S., with about 25 percent belonging to local or state medical societies because of local and state political and licensing considerations; but only about 10 percent belonged to the AMA, with many specialists leaving the organization as their own societies were being formed.[112] There was also the sense that the AMA was run by a small group, who appeared to many to be elitists—and frustration that up to that time, the AMA had failed to influence national health policy.[113]

To address this situation, a committee composed of Drs. J. N. McCormack, P. Maxwell Foshay, and George H. Simmons (newly appointed editor of *JAMA* and Secretary of the AMA) was appointed in 1900 to present suggestions to address these problems at the next yearly meeting. Their charge was to 1) strengthen local and state medical societies, bringing them closer to the national organization; 2) make the organization more attractive to all physicians, including specialists; and 3) enhance the prestige of the organization so as to have a greater effect on national health policy. The committee suggested:

- the creation of a House of Delegates (HOD) that would be the legislative and policy-creating body of the organization, with the board of trustees retaining financial responsibility;

- that most delegates would be from state societies, with others from the various associated groups[114];

- that county societies would be the basic functioning unit of the AMA, with all members automatically belonging to their respective state society;

- that membership in the AMA would no longer be a privilege but a right, open to all Regular (scientifically oriented) physicians; and

- that the AMA should seek to increase membership in each state so as to enhance political activity at both the state and national level, and thereby become a significantly more effective organization.[115]

These suggestions were ratified at the 1901 national meeting; changes to the by-laws followed, and the articles of incorporation modified.[116] These changes were remarkably successful, aided by the aforementioned Dr. McCormack, who in 1903 became a traveling organizer, helping to grow AMA membership from about 10,500 in 1901 to approximately 60,000 in 1906.

The basic structure and purpose of the House of Delegates as the policy-making body of the AMA have remained essentially unchanged since the reorganization in 1901. Quoting from recent publications on the AMA website, "The House of Delegates is the principal policy-making body of the American Medical Association. According to Article VI of the AMA Constitution: The legislative and policy-making body of the Association is the House of Delegates, composed of elected representatives and others as provided in the Bylaws. The House of Delegates shall transact all business of the Association not otherwise specifically provided for in this Constitution and Bylaws, and shall elect the general officers except as otherwise provided in the Bylaws."[117] The House of Delegates is made up of "well over 500 voting delegates (and a corresponding number of alternate delegates), all who are members of the AMA and who have been selected by the organization they represent, such as medical associations (state or territorial), national medical specialty organizations, professional interest medical associations, the five federal services, and several of the AMA's member sections and groups. Some organizations are also allowed to officially observe the proceedings of the HOD, although they are not able to vote."[118][119]

The House of Delegates organization served the AMA well for many decades. Membership numbers continued to grow; members felt they were an integral part of the key decisions made by the organization; and the Association's national influence and prestige greatly increased. After World War II, however, the pace of change in American medicine accelerated. The economy grew at a rapid rate, which increased federal tax revenues; and with these revenues, the U.S. Congress began allocating large sums for medical research through the National Institutes of Health, resulting in great medical advances. The mechanisms of disease were being better understood, and treatments greatly improved. Medical practice was changing rapidly, with an even greater emphasis on specialists (such as internal medicine and surgery) and sub-specialists (such as, nephrology and urology).

But as this research was a national effort, how was society going to ensure that all its citizens would benefit from these tax-funded advances? Would the House of Delegates be creative and imaginative enough to deal with this new reality? Many if not most delegates from the state societies had been active national members for years and were well steeped in AMA tradition, making significant changes in direction difficult. The very size of the HOD and the varied interests of its component members made agreeing on creative responses to new realities a challenge. The AMA has a large entrenched bureaucracy, which by its very nature tends to vigorously oppose significant changes in policy. In a sense, the very success of the pre–World War II HOD structure would make dealing with the challenges after World War II extremely difficult.

Another Major Milestone for the AMA in 1901

Committed to enhancing the development of scientific medicine in the United States, John D. Rockefeller founded the Rockefeller Institute for Medical Research in1901. In the same year, recognizing the AMA as a stalwart of scientifically based medical practice, he gave the Association a $200,000 grant for medical research. Dr. William H. Welch, Dean of the Johns Hopkins School of Medicine, headed the research committee.[120]

To further the AMA's efforts to promote better sanitation, public health, and scientifically based medicine, the Association's committee on national legislation, comprising Drs. H. L. E. Johnson, William H. Welch, and William L. Rodman, had held their first Washington, D.C., meeting in November 1899. They subsequently recruited representatives of the newly formed state societies' legislative committees, and also from the military's health services, to devise a process by which they would coordinate their lobbying efforts. At the first full committee meeting in February 1901, they worked on pending legislation affecting Army and Marine medical services. Lobbying efforts became considerably more effective as the AMA gained in stature after the creation of the House of Delegates. Thus began a lobbying tradition that has continued for over a hundred years.*[121]

   * Lobbying can be a tricky business, however: An organization can lobby for short-term gains, forgoing basic core values and in the long run losing identity and moral standing—and membership.

The AMA and Medical Education

From the beginning of the nineteenth century, the supply of newly graduating physicians to meet the need of our rapidly growing population was grossly inadequate. In addition, prospective students had little money to spend on medical education. In response, enterprising physicians opened many "propriety" schools, with little attention to student qualifications or adequate teaching resources. The result was that a student could quickly receive a medical degree with little quality control and for little cost. When a few thoughtful schools attempted to increase both their standards of admission and the difficulty of the curriculum, as at Yale University in 1825, its student body began to shrink and it had to abandon this attempt at quality.

This experience was repeated for about seventy-five years, until all schools had to meet certain standards or be forced to close. "As late as 1887 an officer of the Maine State Board of Health had an eight-year-old girl apply in her own handwriting for admission to a number of medical schools. Although she stated that she had none of the requirements for admission, over half the schools accepted her application, several of them assuring her that the examinations for a degree were not difficult."[122] Only the Chicago Medical College, founded in 1863 under the direction of Dr. Nathan Smith Davis, was willing for the faculty to sacrifice dollars to maintain standards, requiring a third year for graduation.[123] Following this example, the new President (1869-1909) of Harvard University, Charles William Eliot, took over the finances of the medical school, lengthened the school year from four months to nine, required oral and written final exams in all departments, and extended the coursework from two to three years. Until then, a student at Harvard Medical School had to pass only five of nine five-minute oral tests to graduate. In 1872, on account of these changes, school enrollment had decreased 43 percent from that in 1870, but President Eliot stayed the course, and shortly thereafter the Universities of Pennsylvania, Syracuse, and Michigan followed.[124] The situation had become so chaotic that by 1900 there were approximately as many "medical schools" in the U.S. as in the rest of the world combined.[125]

The founding of Johns Hopkins University Medical School in 1893 had a profound effect throughout the nation, as it was the first medical school to require a bachelor's degree for admission, had a prominent full-time faculty, and was a leader in research; Hopkins and Harvard were also the first medical schools to require that senior medical students have hospital experience.[126] As graduates of Hopkins medical school began to populate the faculties of major schools throughout the nation, the Hopkins model of a medical school slowly became the national norm.

The cause for women in medicine was greatly enhanced by the work of a group of women in Baltimore. M. Carey Thomas, Mary Garrett, Elizabeth King, and Mary Gwinn had already founded Bryn Mawr College when they decided to take advantage of the financial constraints Johns Hopkins was experiencing in forming its new medical school. Eventually they bequeathed $500,000 to Hopkins Medical School, with the majority donated by Mary Garrett under the condition that women be admitted to the school on an equal basis as men. Those admitted also had to have a bachelor's degree, premedical studies, and some exposure to French and German. Hopkins trustees reluctantly accepted the money and the major condition, and the precedent had been set. Today women make up about 48 percent of students accepted to medical schools in the U.S.[127]

The turning point in AMA efforts to address the chaos in American medical education came with the enhanced national presence of the organization after its reorganization, when it formed the House of Delegates in 1901. Buoyed by this success, in 1902 then president Dr. John A. Wyeth appointed an ad hoc committee of five headed by Dr. Arthur Dean Bevan, Chair of the Committee on Medical Education, to specifically address the proper role that the AMA should play in addressing U.S. medical education. The year after, at the 1903 meeting of the AMA in New Orleans, Dr. Bevan observed that "[t]he American Medical Association was formed for the purpose of elevating standards of medical education in this country . . . your committee believes that this is still one of the important functions of the American Medical Association."[128]

Dr. Bevan was referring back to one of Dr. Nathan Smith Davis's founding statements, calling for a national physician convention that "would be conducive to the elevation of the standard of medical education in the United States."[129] At the AMA's initial national meeting in Philadelphia in 1847, a committee on education was thereupon initiated; Dr. Bevan, with the support of his special ad hoc committee on medical education, now proposed by-laws changes providing that the committee on medical education be reconstituted to become the Council on Medical Education. This new entity would include representatives from the American Association of Medical Colleges and the Southern Medical Association. (The Federation of State Medical Boards joined after its founding in 1912.) The HOD ratified the by-laws changes, and in 1904 the Council was officially organized. As medical knowledge was rapidly increasing, with a corresponding need for hospital-based post-graduate specialty and sub-specialty training, the Council became the Council on Medical Education and Hospitals in 1920. This group spearheaded the AMA's profound effect on medical education in this country.

The Council on Medical Education consisted of five AMA members appointed by the Association's President and ratified by the HOD, along with organizational representatives as mentioned above. The Council was to make an annual report to the HOD and make suggestions as to how the AMA could spearhead improvements in U.S. medical education—and, under the authority of the HOD, carry out these recommendations. The Council was initiated with the appointment of five extremely prominent AMA physicians: W. T. Councilman, Professor of Pathology at Harvard University, Charles H. Frazier, Professor of Surgery at the University of Pennsylvania; Victor C. Vaughan, Dean of the University of Michigan Medical School; and J. A. Witherspoon,

Professor of Medicine at Vanderbilt University, in addition to Dr. Bevan, chairman; who was Professor of Surgery at Rush Medical College. The following year, in 1905, the Council held its first conference on the status of medical education in the U.S. and found it to be grossly lacking as compared with schools in Europe. Many schools admitted students who had not completed high school, and only five required at least two years of college.

The Council focused on the licensing board exams passing rates for students from the various medical schools that was published yearly in the *Journal of the American Medical Association*, starting in 1902. Although the Council created a long-term goal of a curriculum similar to that in England, Germany, and France, in 1905 it set what it considered a minimum standard: four years of high school as preliminary education, four years of medical school, and an acceptable passing rate on state licensing board exams. Using the passing rate on licensing exams, which were now used throughout the country (see Chapter 4), as an objective criterion of medical school proficiency, the Council published tables dividing medical schools into four categories: Class I, less than 10 percent failures; Class II, 10-20 percent failures; Class III, greater than 20 percent failures; and Class IV, fewer than ten graduates or other unusual circumstances. Publication of these revised criteria would appear in *JAMA* in 1908.[130]

The Council recognized that although board passage rates were objective criteria, more was needed to accurately describe the value of education at a particular medical school. The Council accordingly created ten measures, each assigned a value of ten points that would require visiting every school for evaluation. They were:

1) the passing rate on state board exams,

2) the requirements of preliminary (pre-med) education,

3) the medical school's curriculum,

4) the school's physical facility,

5) laboratories, and the instruction associated with them,

6) outpatient facilities, with appropriate instruction

7) hospital facility, with appropriate over-site

8) full-time faculty for the first two years, with evidence of research,

9) negative points for any profit motive, and

10) a library, a pathological specimens museum, and teaching equipment.

Pursuant to their evaluation, schools were then classified into three groups, according to points earned: Class A, above 70 points, acceptable; Class B, between 50 and 70 points, doubtful; and Class C, below 50 points, unacceptable.* A member of the Council, usually accompanied by the Council secretary, Dr. N. P. Colwell, then visited every medical school.

> * I believe medical school accrediting agencies need to do further serious reevaluation of criteria in light of the need to decrease the cost of a medical education while still maintaining quality, encouraging compassion, and teaching integrative thinking.

Inspections/evaluations began in 1906, and the process was published in *JAMA* in 1907.[131] Of the 160 medical schools then in the U.S., 82 were classified as class A, 46 as class B, and 32 as class C. These results were presented to the HOD in 1907, with each medical school privately made aware of its grade. Although the grades were not made public, the survey had a marked effect on the schools, with many making changes to meet the criteria and others closing. Within a short period of time, the 160 medical schools in the U.S. became less than 100. Twenty homeopathic and ten eclectic schools were included in the review, but as the requirement of undergraduate science requirements became standard, their application numbers dwindled, in essence forcing them to close.

The Need for an Independent, Unbiased Review

In December 1908, the Council, sensing that medical colleges were questioning the Council's objectivity in evaluating medical school quality, decided to ask the prestigious Carnegie Foundation for the Advancement of Teaching to participate in a new, independent study. The foundation eagerly accepted the invitation and assigned Dr. Abraham Flexner to be in charge. Dr. N. P. Colwell, Secretary of the Council, assisted him; they visited every medical school in the United States and Canada beginning in 1908 and published what became known as the Flexner report in 1910.[132] The Flexner report ratified and expanded the requirements enumerated by the Council in its rating system.

By 1927, the number of medical schools in the U.S. was half the number—80 versus 160 in 1905 - as the requirements for acceptance were greatly enhanced. The proportion of Class A schools increased, while the proportions of schools in the other categories significantly decreased. This rather astonishing accomplishment of the Council was made possible by the voluntary involvement of the Carnegie Foundation and the full support of the AMA, the state licensing boards, and the Association of American Medical Colleges (AAMC). There was no need to resort to the force of law. There was however, justifiable concern that with the closing of many medical schools, the supply of qualified physicians would decrease. In 1905 5,606 students graduated from 160 medical schools, whereas in 1922, there were only 2,529 graduates. By 1944, however, that number had increased to 5,163, close to the graduating number in 1905.[133] And in the late 1930s there was an influx of physicians from Europe escaping the threat posed by Nazi Germany.[134] Accelerating the curriculum increased the number of physicians graduating from American medical schools during World War II; but with about a third of the nations' physicians participating in the war effort, there was nonetheless a severe shortage on the home front.*[135]

---

* The number of physicians needed to meet the needs of the American population has always been a difficult question, and is especially so under the now artificial market conditions (see Chapter 4). Federal government financial support for medical schools in ways affecting physician output has taken various forms over the years, beginning with the Health Professions Education Assistance Act of 1963; see P. P. Reynolds, "A Legislative History of Federal Assistance for Health Professionals Training in Primary Care Medicine and Dentistry in the United States, 1963-2008," *Academic Medicine* 2008: 83, 1004-14. The AMA role in this effort has been significant, and is reviewed in detail by F. D. Campion in *The AMA and U.S. Health Policy since 1940* (Chicago Review Press, 1984), chapter 14: "A Liberalized Policy on Federal Aid to Education," pp. 234-44. The problems of matching post-graduate residency training slots with increasing numbers of U.S. medical school graduates is reviewed by J. K. Iglehart in "The Residency Mismatch," *New England Journal of Medicine* 2013: 369, 297-99. Two other articles in the *New England Journal of Medicine* highlight the difficulties in addressing U.S. physician manpower needs: J. K. Iglehart, "Grassroots Activism and the Pursuit of an Expanded Physician Supply," *New England Journal of Medicine* 2008: 358, 1741-49, and D. C. Goodman and E. S. Fisher, "Physician Workforce Crisis? Wrong Diagnosis, Wrong Prescription," *New England Journal of Medicine* 2008: 358, 1658-61.

The funding of sufficient medical school clinical faculty to educate the proper number of students was and continues to be a challenge. In response to the Flexner report, the Rockefeller Foundation started the transition of clinical faculty from part-time to full-time status by awarding a million-dollar grant to the Johns Hopkins Medical School for that purpose in 1913. In 1924, Flexner reviewed medical schools and found that considerable progress had been made: full-time faculty was teaching Basic courses, and a four-year curriculum with adequate clinical faculty was in place.[*]

[*] With some variations on the theme and given the reality of vastly increased scientific knowledge, the four-year medical school curriculum is now standard. Over the years, financial constraints have caused the initiation of other means of financing clinical faculty, such as practice plans, faculty clinics, and geographic full-time status, in essence private practice located at the school. The changing financial situation in medicine at this time, characterized by escalating medical costs, has made the financial arrangements of clinical faculty progressively more complex.

The AMA also successfully established itself as the upholder of standards for acceptable post–medical school physician training. In 1914, the Council on Medical Education declared standards for hospital training of young physicians during their first post-graduate year. The AMA then published a list of approved programs. There is no doubt that not being on that list has meant little or no likelihood of attracting recruits to that program.

Little understood by the public is the importance of young physician training programs to a hospital. Residency programs afford prestige to a hospital as a teaching center. Residents provide physician services at a far reduced cost, with many subsequently joining the medical staff after their training. The hospital also attracts teachers for these trainees who are among the brightest in the community, enhancing the hospital's prestige. Training programs thus help in the recruitment of excellent physicians and in improving care, thereby making the hospital more attractive to patients. As training programs are largely funded by federal and other sources, thus making them an outstanding investment for the hospital.

The AMA, by its membership on various certifying boards is prominent in post–medical school training in the specialties of medicine and surgery, initially called residencies, to be completed after internship. The internship year has since been merged into the residency process, with a transitional year, called a transitional residency, added before some specialty areas, such as radiology and anesthesia. In 1927, the AMA Council on Medical Education and Hospitals published its approved list for residency training. In 1934, the Council, along with the Advisory Board of Medical Specialties (later called the American Board of Medical Specialties), officially recognized specialty boards such as the American Board of Internal Medicine and the American Board of Surgery. These boards administer the testing of physicians as they complete their training in these specialties and declare them to be board-certified if they are successful. This has become a rite of passage and confers added prestige on the physician, which in turn means more patients, more income, and higher status in the physician community.

The Council remained active after the issuance of the Flexner report and published several narratives on the progress of medical schools as they strived to meet standards. Concern for the status of medical education after the Great Depression led to a comprehensive survey of the eighty-nine medical schools in the U.S. and Canada between 1934 and 1936. This survey was conducted by the Dean of the Syracuse University School of Medicine, Dr. H. G. Weiskotten, who was also serving as Chair of the Council. The purpose of the survey (unlike that of the Flexner report) was not to close weak for-profit institutions that had by this time disappeared, but rather to help the schools recover from the stresses of the Depression, with constructive criticism provided where appropriate.

In 1942, the AMA and the AAMC formed a liaison committee that would meet biannually to facilitate closer cooperation with respect to all future issues regarding North American medical schools. Because of its expertise in the area medical education, the Council also assists, when asked, in evaluating the training of allied health practitioners such as nurses, physical therapists, and radiological and clinical laboratory technicians.

The prestige of the Flexner Report was such that Flexner himself was able to convince the Rockefeller Foundation to grant almost fifty million dollars to the schools rated as worthwhile. Other foundations followed suit, strengthening the stronger schools while forcing the weaker ones out of existence. America was now a major industrial nation, medical advances were proceeding at an accelerated pace, laboratories and faculty were larger and more expensive, precluding the existence of the proprietary medical school.

The need to include more information into the medical school curriculum because of the ever-expanding scientific knowledge base, has given rise to questions regarding proper content including that of the humanities. In addition, the greatly increased funding of medical research on the part of the federal government and others has led to a marked expansion of the research efforts at research-oriented medical schools, and also helped to increase the number of medical schools, from 87 in 1967 to 127 in 1993, and 141 U.S. and 17 Canadian accredited schools in 2013.[136] [137] As the federal government has experienced financial difficulties, however, research funding has recently decreased in inflationary adjusted dollars; these same schools face serious adjustment issues owing to large fixed costs and research faculty.[*] Adding to medical school costs has been the expansion of the curriculum, including the history of medicine[138] and, especially, medical ethics—which has assumed increased importance as technology has created new and difficult situations, especially at the end of life.[139] Another difficult problem is the underrepresentation of minorities as physicians in the U.S.[†]

[*] The problem is exacerbated by our out-of-control costs for medical school education: Many if not most physicians graduating from medical school have incurred hundreds of thousands of dollars of debt. Surely it is time for a careful re-evaluation of the medical school curriculum so as to achieve excellent training while seriously decreasing costs. During the first two years, the collective student body should be responsible only for the proportion of time during which a single scientist or equivalent teacher from each of the basic departments spends actual time in contact with students. I believe this teaching should be focused around cases available in the literature—for example, in the *New England Journal of Medicine.* The last two clinical years of medical school actually cost the school very little, as teaching is done by clinical faculty who are being compensated via their patient care responsibilities and residents who are mostly funded by the Federal Government. Some costs do apply, in connection with tracking students' progress and providing special lectures where indicated; there are fixed overhead costs, but these should be minimal, especially if amortized over many years. I believe that, given careful review and curriculum restructuring, medical school costs could be approximately halved without sacrificing quality.

[†] This difficulty starts with our grossly inadequate public education system, which in this country lags behind that of many other nations, with a huge divergence between achievers and underachievers. [140]

As medical science has continued its relentless onslaught to reveal the secrets of nature and given an ever-expanding technology, new specialties and sub-specialties of medicine continue to be created. Training in all of these areas, and in primary care, takes place *after* the four years of medical school. Specialty boards continue to be created under the auspices of the AMA, and have created tests in each area to certify acquisition of the knowledge and skills necessary to provide quality care. (See Chapter 4.) Accrediting agencies are charged with extensively reviewing each program to evaluate curriculum, faculty, and training. Residency and fellowship (sub-specialty training) programs undergo intensive review by the various residency (and fellowship) review committees under the auspices of the Accreditation Council for Graduate Medical Education (ACGME; see http://www.acgme.org/acgmeweb/).

In summary, starting in the early twentieth century, the AMA, along with other voluntary organizations, was able to transform medicine from a trade to a respected profession. This transformation took place without the force of law, but was built on the 1889 Supreme Court ruling that medical licensure was in the best interests of the public. (See Chapter 4.) The challenge we face today is that the infrastructure built to ensure the competency of our profession has become too complex, requiring an ever more expensive medical educational system. Not all medical schools need to be proficient in basic medical research. Certainly many of the less well-endowed schools could specialize in clinical studies, which could be funded by the National Institutes of Health. We need to streamline our accrediting bureaucracy, while emphasizing the humanity of our profession and the special skills needed to maximally integrate the science and art of medicine.

6
Issues of Access and Insurance, 1913–64
The AMA Fails To Lead

"Sickness" Insurance — If Only!

In 1883, German Chancellor Otto von Bismarck initiated a Health Insurance Bill. It provided for mandatory insurance, but applied only to low-income workers and a few government employees.[141] The British Chancellor of the Exchequer and later prime minister David Lloyd George, after visiting Germany in 1908, was instrumental in creating the 1911 National Insurance Act, which applied to a restricted set of low-wage earners and also provided maternity benefits for the disadvantaged.[142] This European effort was not lost on Theodore Roosevelt's short-lived American Progressive Party, which in the course of his unsuccessful bid for the presidency in 1912, proposed a form of national health insurance.[143] Aware of the social issues involved, in 1913 the AMA Council on Health and Public Instruction suggested sending an employee to Europe to study these fledgling plans for compulsory sickness insurance. The AMA Board of Trustees did not agree and referred the matter back to the Council.*[144]

> * Thus marks the beginning of the AMA's hundred-year inability to propose innovative solutions to provide universal access while at the same time maintaining the ability to develop a true therapeutic relationship with the patient without bureaucratic oversight and interference—a relationship that I believe is crucial to developing patient trust and physician continuity, which results in better and more cost effective care. Later we will see that as central planning and bureaucracy grow, so do fragmented care and cost.

Two years later, the Judicial Council of the AMA presented to the full House of Delegates a thoughtful essay on the increasing American attention to social programs for the disadvantaged. The Council took note of the growth of European compulsory sickness insurance, and reported its impression that the German system had experienced problems in maintaining medical quality and assuring free choice of a physician. The report concluded "[t]he medical profession will accept its responsibility in these new social conditions as it has always accepted its responsibilities in the past." The report was referred to the appropriate Reference Committee, which punted by referring it to the state societies.[145]

Noting that in 1916, the state legislatures of New York and Massachusetts were considering bills on sickness insurance, the AMA Board of Trustees authorized and funded a special committee made up of members of the Council on Health and Public Instruction and the Judicial Council. They were tasked to carefully study the issue and present a plan. Under the leadership of Dr. Alexander Lambert, the committee hired staff and a year later produced an extensive thirty-five-page report. It assumed that national sickness insurance was soon to come about and wished to avoid the conflicts between the medical profession and the government that occurred with the passing of the National Insurance Act in Great Britain. The committee opposed voluntary insurance, feeling that compulsory state insurance was the only way to benefit the neediest groups. Its report favored the German plan, noting, "[h]owever one may criticize the details, the [German] insurance act has unquestionably improved the health of the working class which has come under the law."[146]

California and Massachusetts state societies reported favorably on sickness insurance, and bills were pending in fourteen other states. The special committee observed "[t]here is no question that the enormous modern industrial development has increased the hazards of the wage earner and has increased also the dependence of a large part of the population on their own physical well-being and working capacity. This country today still possesses the strongest development of individualism, but so great has been the collective development of industry and so strong the collective development of labor that the collective protection of the individual against a universal hazard has found ready and vigorous support. . . . Blind opposition, indignant repudiation, bitter denunciation of these laws is worse than useless; it leaves nowhere and it leaves the profession in a position of helplessness if the rising tide of social development sweeps over them." This last statement from the committee was in response to the condemnation of these ideas of insurance in the *Boston Medical and Surgical Journal* and the opposition voiced by many state societies. In response to the perceived need of social insurance the House of Delegates passed a resolution supporting the committee's suggestions, with the caveats that any supported legislation should provide for freedom of choice of physician, payment of the physician proportional to the work provided, separation of physician and non-physician duties, and medical professionals being a member of the appropriate administrative bodies.[147]

Looming over these high ideals, however, was World War I, and amidst the resultant turmoil, the fervor for sickness insurance seemed to lose its steam, while those opposed remained adamant. In 1919, Dr. Lambert, now president-elect of the AMA, reacted strongly to the growing organized campaign against the concept of sickness insurance. In the following year, 1920, there was a flurry of attacks on sickness insurance in both the national AMA journal and in various state medical journals. Some of this anger was directed at I. M. Rubinow, Ph.D., the secretary of the subcommittee on social insurance of the Council on Health and Public Instruction, who many thought had a conflict of interest: While employed by the AMA, he was also an employee of the American Association for Labor Legislation, a major lobby for sickness insurance. At the 1920 HOD meeting, the Illinois, Michigan, and New York state delegations introduced a resolution against any compulsory sickness insurance provided, controlled, or regulated by any state or by the federal government. The Reference Committee on Hygiene and Public Health concurred, and the HOD passed the following resolution, which became AMA policy for the next forty-five years: "That the American Medical Association declares its opposition to the institution of any plan embodying the system of compulsory contributory insurance against illness, or any other plan of compulsory insurance which provides for medical service to be rendered contributors or their dependents, provided, controlled or regulated by any state or federal government."[148] This was an especially ironic resolution, as Dr. Lambert, a champion of sickness insurance, was at the time President of the AMA.*

> * This resolution ignored the sweeping social changes so eloquently described by Dr. Lambert. There was no attempt to enunciate a counterproposal proposing a compromise position that would provide care for the needy yet eliminate interference from third parties. The lack of this alternative has plagued this nation ever since.

Why the radical change of direction with regard to sickness insurance over such a relatively short period of time? Noticing now the discontent of so many physicians with the present-day practice of medicine, we can understand the apprehension of those 1920s physicians to government-dominated and -controlled medicine. The AMA leadership at the time did not understand the strength of the conviction of American physicians that this was not Europe, and that a uniquely American solution to care for the poor was needed, which would not be an easy task.

Historians speculate on the reasons for the 1920 rebuke of sickness insurance. World War I and then the failure of the League of Nations had led to a distrust of European liberalism. The medical profession was also changing, and with the more stringent requirements to enter medical school (see Chapter 5), students came from more middle- and upper-class families, who tended to have a more conservative political philosophy. And perhaps rising physician incomes between 1916 and 1919 made doctors less inclined to risk the possible adverse effects of third-party patient-doctor interference.[149] I would add that the House of Delegates relished the idea of demonstrating to the officers and the Board that it too had power to affect policy.

Whatever It Is, We're Against It

In 1922, the AMA was strong in its opposition to the Sheppard-Towner Maternity and Infancy Act of 1921.[150] In the early 1920s, childbirth was the second leading cause of death among women. The death rate among children was about 20 percent in the first year of life and about 33 percent in the first five years, and these rates were more severe among the poor. Sheppard-Towner provided for federal matching funds to the states to create health clinics for women, to hire physicians and nurses to educate and provide medical care for these women and children, and to enable midwife training along with nutrition and cleanliness instruction. It was signed into law by President Warren Harding and was sponsored in Congress by Senator Morris Sheppard (D-Texas) and Representative Horace Towner (R-Iowa). At the 1922 HOD meeting in St. Louis, the President of the AMA, Dr. Hubert Work, set forth the principles behind the AMA's objection to the law. "The public is entitled to know the legitimate limitations of a state's participation in the practice of medicine. . . . Promiscuous medical treatment of disease . . . is not a state's function, and interference with it through any unit of government should not be tolerated by the public or by physicians. . . . The practice of medicine must remain a process of personal contact, invoking the patient's right of selection and the direct moral responsibility of the physician, with a sympathetic reaction between the two."[151] A challenge to the Act's constitutionality, however, failed at the Supreme

Court in 1923. Thus, the first federally sponsored social welfare program did meet Constitutional standards.[152]

> * This statement is as true today as it was in 1922. But it does not rule out, as the AMA maintained at that time, the provision of life-saving care for women and children. A possible compromise might have been having the states provide a voucher, or some other form of financial support, for services, with start-up grants for the clinics if necessary. In this way the patient-doctor relationship would have been totally maintained without state bureaucratic interference. Certainly the AMA should have made counter-proposals to meet its obligation to care for those who desperately needed it. Unfortunately for all concerned, this did not happen.

The Federal Government Provided Care for Certain Groups for Centuries

Wars have played a major role in American history. With wars come casualties and the obligation of the nation to care for the wounded and disabled. Casualties alone for all our wars, excluding deaths, number approximately 1.5 million.[153] Starting in the early 1800s, the federal government created marine hospitals for merchant seamen, run by what is now called the U.S. Public Health Service.[154] The U.S. Naval Home, founded in Philadelphia in 1812, was the first national facility to provide medical care for disabled veterans. The Soldiers' Home, built in 1851 and St. Elizabeth's Hospital, built in 1855, both in Washington D.C., expanded our nation's capacity to care for those disabled by our early wars. In his Second Inaugural Address in 1865, Abraham Lincoln is often quoted as exhorting the nation "to bind up the nation's wounds, to care for him who shall have borne the battle and for his widow and his orphan."* Because of the large number of disabled veterans after the Civil War, in 1865 the National Asylum for Disabled Volunteer Soldiers was founded to provide room, board, and medical care to disabled and indigent veterans regardless of whether their disabilities were service-related.

> * This is the motto of the present-day Veterans Administration—certainly a valid one, but could it in many cases be more efficient and easier for veterans to have financial support for care within their communities?

During and Immediately after World War I, most care for the wounded was provided at military hospitals. By 1919, it had become obvious that additional medical resources would be needed, and Congress authorized the U.S. Public Health Service to provide care for the overflow from military hospitals. This law authorized the building of new hospitals, along with the transfer of a few military facilities. The workload was so great that the law also provided for the use of private hospitals via contract.[155] The Veterans' Bureau, founded in 1921, was an attempt to consolidate veterans' affairs, and in 1922 it took over control of the U.S. Public Health Service hospitals that were caring for veterans. In 1923 the first hospital for black veterans was built, in Tuskegee, Alabama.[156]

In 1923, the Veterans' Bureau petitioned the AMA for its physicians to have the same status as military doctors; as members they would have a representative in the House of Delegates. But it was not until 1945, with the reorganization of the VA hospital system to correct what the AMA thought was the lower standards of VA hospitals that this request was granted.[157] The AMA opposed the construction of additional VA hospitals in 1924 and 1933 because they offered care to veterans with non-service-connected disabilities.[158] [159] In 1933 the AMA wanted those veterans to seek care in hospitals and physicians of their own choosing.*

> * There appears to be some logic to this stance; however a pattern was developing whereby the AMA made no counter-proposal. Perhaps a means-tested voucher could have been suggested.

Group Health Plans

In 1929, Justin Ford Kimball, working at Baylor University in Houston, Texas, developed a plan whereby schoolteachers were provided twenty-one days of hospital care for six dollars per year. He needed and obtained a critical mass of participants to be able to fund the few who needed hospitalization each year.[160] Just ten years later, however, the number of participants had grown from about 1,300 participants initially to approximately 3 million nationwide.[161] This was the beginning of Blue Cross. In the Pacific Northwest, around 1,900 mining companies began to provide medical care for their workers. To accomplish this, they paid monthly fees to "medical service bureaus" made up of physician groups. These plans were the forerunners of Blue Shield, first founded in California in 1939.[162]

The AMA's reaction to these newer ways of funding medical care was not positive, as illustrated by this 1930 quote from the AMA Judicial Council, "With regard to the practice of medicine by corporations, it is the opinion of the Judicial Council, based on present evidence, that such practice is detrimental to the best interest of scientific medicine and of the people themselves. When medical service is made impersonal, when the humanities of medicine are removed, when the coldness and automaticity of the machine are substituted for the humane interest inherent in individual service and the professional and scientific independence of the individual physician, the greatest incentive to scientific improvement will be destroyed and the public will be poorly served.'"[163]

* Medicine must be personal, individualized, and caring, with adequate time to spend with each patient. The development of a therapeutic relationship is important. Ideally, when the patient has a direct financial relationship with the physician, the odds are probably higher that a trusting therapeutic relationship will occur. The mining companies in the Pacific Northwest could have given their workers vouchers (a completely new concept at that time) to be used to pay for their medical care rather than putting the physicians on salary. But the AMA did not recommend that action as a remedy to their objection to corporate medicine. Instead, their objection to corporate or third party medicine was so strong because of their fear that this mechanism of payment would detract from the patient-doctor relationship and third party financial issues would lead to bureaucratically controlled medicine. But, again the AMA did not lead by presenting alternatives

Because of the extreme conditions caused by the economic depression of the 1930's, group hospitalization and individual hospital insurance plans did gain traction. But the Judicial Council of the AMA thought that this trend constituted an attempt by hospitals to collect full payment, especially because of the decrease in endowment income and public contributions. The Council's concern was that salaried physicians would become servants of hospital's finances; therefore, it believed, physicians should separate themselves from hospitals.*[164]

* Easier said than done, when so many patients did not have the funds to pay the physician directly—and the AMA made no effort to try to deal with that underlying problem. It is one thing to uphold the appropriate underlying principle that an intimate patient-physician relationship is critical to good care, but quite another to provide creative ideas as to how to implement that principle in times of severe financial distress.

There was dissent within a loosely affiliated AMA committee regarding third-party participation in medical services. The independently financed Committee on the Cost of Medical Care, chaired by a former President of both the AMA and Stanford University, published both a majority and minority report. The majority report supported the increase in contract practice, while the minority report was against this. With approval from the AMA's Board of Trustees, Dr. Morris Fishbein, then editor of *JAMA*, wrote a commentary on this report, praising the minority viewpoint while castigating the majority's findings.*[165]

> * The leadership of the AMA could not reconcile its fear of third-party partici-pation in medical care with the needs of the less fortunate, which during the Depression represented a very large portion of the American population.

Social Security with or without Health Insurance

The election of Franklin D. Roosevelt in 1932 marked a turning point in American history. This election confirmed the idea that government was to have a more active role in American life. Would the new President push for comprehensive health coverage as part of his Social Security law?

On June 29, 1934, the President issued an executive order establish-ing a Committee on Economic Security. The committee was composed of several cabinet officers and high government officials along with an administrative director, college professor and economist Wilbur J. Witte. As administrative director, Professor Witte wrote the commit-tee's report to the President, and he is considered the "father of Social Security."[166]

Frances Perkins, the Secretary of the Interior, requested that a Med-ical Advisory Committee be appointed to study just how the proposed new law should address health care. Dr. Walter L. Bierring, President of the AMA, was appointed to the committee, along with Dr. Harvey Cushing as committee chair. In accepting this chairmanship, Dr. Cush-ing noted to Secretary Perkins that previously the government had been advised by non-physicians who had no knowledge of the practice of medicine or of the importance of the intimacy of the patient-physician relationship. A great deal was made of the fact that Dr. Cushing's daugh-ter, Betsy, was married to President and Eleanor Roosevelt's oldest son, James. It is known that Dr. Cushing and the President did exchange cor-respondence on the matter, and the President did mention that this was not the time to consolidate the various federal health agencies.[167]

Dr. Cushing's Medical Advisory Committee report was sent to President Roosevelt on January 15, 1935. Before, in early January the AMA Board of Trustees had called a special meeting of the House of Delegates for February 15, 1935, to discuss compulsory health insurance. This meeting was called to formally vote to putting the AMA on record against the Wagner Bill, which placed health affairs under a nonmedical board in the Department of Labor, and its companion, the Epstein Bill, proposing sickness insurance in the individual states. This was in spite of President Roosevelt's having sent a message to Congress that "I am not at this time recommending the adoption of so-called 'health insurance,' although groups representing the medical profession are cooperating with the federal government in further study of the subject and definite progress is being made."[168]

At this special meeting, the House of Delegates reaffirmed opposition to all forms of compulsory sickness insurance—though the California Medical Society did support compulsory sickness insurance for that state. A few months later, at the regular HOD meeting, AMA President Dr. Walter Bierring observed that "[i]n certain social and economic security measures introduced in Congress, all reference to health sickness insurance was eliminated, and bills proposing plans for compulsory health insurance presented in one or two state legislatures were unsuccessful and did not even come up for passage."*[169]

> * One can guess that at that regular 1935 HOD meeting, the delegates and officers of the AMA were feeling pretty proud of having stopped any form of state- or federally funded health care. But for a collection of really bright people, they showed little imagination. Where were the counterproposals? Why were they stuck on defeating European models of state involvement, instead of proposing other ways whereby the state could ensure that all have access to health care while at the same time preventing state incursion into the examining room?

The Social Security Act of August 14, 1935 [H.R. 7260], was composed of eleven titles: Grants to States for Old-Age Assistance, Federal Old Age Benefits, Grants to States for Unemployment Compensation Administration, Grants to States for Aid to Dependent Children, Grants to States for Maternal and Child Welfare, Public Health Work, Social Security Board, Taxes with Respect to Employment, Tax on Employers of Eight or More, Grants to States for Aid to the Blind, and General Provisions.[170] The Act thus provided for only a few medical benefits and excluded sickness insurance, which to the AMA constituted a profound victory.[171]

1943: A Seminal Year for the American Medical Association and Organized Medicine

In 1938, the U.S. Justice Department sought an indictment against the AMA and a few other medical organizations; the editor of *JAMA*, Dr. Morris Fishbein; and the Secretary-General Manager of the AMA, Dr. Olin West, on anti-trust charges. Organized medicine was charged with preventing salaried physicians of the Group Health Association of Washington, D.C., a prepaid health insurance plan, from acquiring hospital privileges. The case wound its way through the court system, and eventually, in 1943, the U.S. Supreme Court found the AMA and the District of Columbia Medical Society, but no individuals, guilty of anti-trust behavior. The fines imposed were small, but the verdict had a chilling effect on some, especially Dr. West, with respect to AMA political activity. Still, when Senators Robert Wagner (D-NY) and James Murray (D-MT) along with Congressman John Dingell (D-MI) submitted their 1943 bill, calling for compulsory health insurance for all Americans to be added to the Social Security law, the AMA House of Delegates put aside any lobbying reservations. The HOD formed the powerful Council on Medical Service and Public Relations as a standing committee complete with funding, thus bypassing the authority of the Board of Trustees. At the same time, a Washington, D.C. lobbying office was authorized that became operative the following year.

The AMA had already changed its position and was now supporting voluntary prepaid hospital insurance. But the Association was still strongly opposed to a government-centered health care system in the U.S. such as was being proposed in Great Britain. The National Physicians' Committee for the Extension of Medical Services, a loosely affiliated group headed by a former President of the AMA, Dr. Edward H. Cary, raised significant money and actively propagandized against *any* government role in medicine. This group was active for a decade beginning in 1938.[172] While World War II was still raging, the Wagner-Murray-Dingell bill had no chance of serious consideration, but it certainly was a strong signal of the growing sentiment favoring universal access to medical care in the United States.*

* The Association should have sensed that those wanting all Americans to have access to good health care were probably on the right side of history. Besides, having all Americans insured could be financially rewarding for physicians. The real threat was a bureaucratic government-dominated system that would threaten the therapeutic close relationship between patient and physician. Recognizing that that was the problem, the AMA should have started thinking of ways to meet both concerns i.e. funding directly to the individual.. This was a failure of creative thinking, locked in to a preconceived notion.

The Next Challenge: 1945

The Wagner-Murray-Dingell bill was reintroduced in May 1945.[173] A more comprehensive version of the 1943 bill, it created national social insurance providing for health insurance for all and federalized unemployment insurance in addition to greater old age and survivor benefits. These benefits were to be administered and financed by an expanded Social Security System. Opposition to this plan came quickly from many sources: the AMA, the American Hospital Association, Protestant and Catholic hospitals, the American Dental Association, the American Bar Association, the Chamber of Commerce, the National Grange, and the American Farm Bureau Federation. Complicating the opposition to this revised law was President Harry S. Truman's message to Congress in November 1945. The President called for every American to have "the right to adequate medical care and the opportunity to achieve and enjoy good health and the right to adequate protection from the economic fears of sickness." At that time he also proposed an expansion of Social Security to fund and administer expanded health care coverage.[174]

Senate hearings for the Wagner-Murray-Dingell bill began in April 1946, but by June, despite the President's support, the bill was dead in committee. Wagner, Murray, and Dingell again introduced their bill in 1946, after the Republicans had won control of Congress, but again to no avail. This time, Republican Senators Robert Taft (R-OH), Howard Smith (R-NJ), and Joseph Ball (R -MN) submitted a health bill limiting comprehensive governmental health insurance to the poor. Murray and Wagner, along with other Democrats, strongly opposed any form of means-tested* approach, resulting in Taft pulling his bill. [†175] It should be noted that the AMA actually supported a few of the suggestions President Truman proposed in his November 1945 message to Congress, such as federal monies for the building of hospitals and health centers under the Hill-Burton Act and development of a National Science Foundation under the direction of a scientific board.

* Providing the benefit for only those below a predetermined income.

† In retrospect, both Taft and the AMA could have championed their conservative principles at this time by proposing tax-based health insurance premium support as a means of meeting this important social need; Individuality would thereby have been maintained with little intrusion by government bureaucracy. But instead, *both* parties proposed a government-centered approach to health care; at that time they differed only in the extent or size of the program. The major Western democracies have been and still seem limited in their approach to universal health care coverage by the 1883 precedent set in Germany by Otto von Bismarck; the concept of providing citizens with the necessary funds to secure their own health care did not appear on the scene until half a century later. The battle rages today: a defined benefit involving the government bureaucracy versus a defined payment revolving around individuals along with price transparency so that patient & doctor could develop more efficient and personal methods of delivering health care.

Elections Are Not Over 'til They're Over: 1948

Most people in 1948 thought they would get a respite from the sanctimony and self-righteousness of both sides in the raging health care debate.[176] The election of Republican Thomas E. Dewey was thought to be a certainty, and so health care would not again be a burning issue. Dewey's biggest problem was being the leader of the liberal wing of the party as opposed to Robert Taft, leader of the conservative wing and from Ohio, a must state for Dewey—which he lost. In the end, Truman campaigned harder and with more substance than Dewey, focused on the issue of national mandatory health care, and barely won a term as President in his own right and not because he had been Roosevelt's Vice President.[177]

After Truman's victory, the proponents of voluntary insurance, buoyed by the growth of health insurance as a work benefit, and the proponents of compulsory insurance through the Social Security Act quickly rallied their respective forces for the battle ahead. The AMA reiterated its belief in voluntary prepayment plans, calling compulsory national health insurance a step toward "socialism," an often-charged label that was really invoking the inefficiencies of central planning and a mammoth bureaucracy. The word "socialism" at that time was quite emotional, owing to the spreading threat of Communism. The AMA expanded its Washington office, hired a public relations firm, and assessed its members $25 each to support its position in the political arena. Meanwhile, compulsory government insurance was being advocated by President Truman, who appointed the chief of the Federal Security Agency (later Health, Education, and Welfare; still later, Health and Human Services), Oscar R. Ewing.* Proponents of mandatory national insurance included organized labor, a few small physician groups, and the Committee for National Health, financed by Mary Lasker, wife of the advertising executive Albert D. Lasker.

> * An example of how an entrenched bureaucracy truly believes in dedication to its mission, and in its expansion to solve the problems of society. As the funding of a federal department is almost guaranteed, it can continually champion its own cause. An editorial in the *St. Louis Globe-Democrat* questioned the propriety of a large agency of the federal government using taxpayer dollars to influence Congressional action. The true debate is not regarding the existence of the federal bureaucracy, but rather its proper place and size in our society.

The AMA, besides building a financial war chest, decided to present to the American people a much more professional campaign than anything it had done in the past. It fired its old warhorse, Dr. Morris Fishbein, whose acidic attacks on mandatory national health insurance had grown thin, and hired the polished public relations firm of Whitaker and Baxter, which had a proven track record on the issue, as they had helped the California Medical Association defeat Governor Earl Warren's 1945 plan for a state-funded health insurance program. It used editorials in the printed press, radio spots, letters to Congressmen, speaker's bureaus, and millions of pamphlets, along with recruiting many other groups to its cause—all touting the virtues of expanding voluntary insurance and the dangers of mandated national insurance. Although President Truman supported mandatory national health insurance, his public discussions were circumspect, as he had doubts about the financial implications of such a program.

Those supporting national mandatory health insurance focused their efforts in Congress on the Murray-Dingell revised bill (Wagner had retired) they hoped to bring to the floor in late April 1949. But the steam was out of the movement. Voluntary health insurance had grown tremendously as a viable alternative that was favored by the public. Critical organizations such as the Catholic Church, the American Legion, women's clubs, and others all supported voluntary insurance. The revised bill never made it out of committee, as Republicans and Southern Democrats rallied together at the committee level. The Republicans, now a minority party in Congress, proposed alternatives to the Murray-Dingell bill; one was coverage for the poor requiring a means test for coverage. The bill having the best chance of passage was the bipartisan Hill-Aiken bill,[178] which proposed subsidies to the states to help the poor pay for private insurance such as Blue Cross. This bill had Republican and Southern Democratic support along with that of the AMA and the American Hospital Association, as well as more public support than Murray-Dingell. President Truman apparently felt obliged to stick with the compulsory national insurance supported by his liberal constituency and would not support Hill-Aiken.[179] This inability to compromise prevented Truman from expanding health care to the poor during the first year of the 81st Congress.[180]

In August 1949, President Truman proposed that the Federal Security Agency headed by Oscar Ewing be elevated to a cabinet position. This would have lent more prestige to Ewing and a bigger platform from which to move Murray-Dingell out of committee, for a vote on the floor. The AMA led the political fight against this move, which was easily defeated in the Senate, 62-30, and a year later in the House, 249-71. Truman planned an all-out campaign for pro–national health insurance candidates in the elections of 1950, hoping to change the complexion of Congress enough so that it would support Murray-Dingell. But the Korean conflict prevented him from intensive campaigning and the election resulted in significant Democrat losses: although the party still retained control of Congress, many advocates of national insurance were defeated—and with this defeat, Truman gave up on Congress's passing national mandatory health insurance.[181] But Truman and Ewing persisted by creating the President's Commission on the Health Needs of the Nation, whose mission was to recommend possible future legislation. Its suggestions included the forerunners of Medicare and Medicaid, both of which are government- and bureaucracy-centered as opposed to funding individually centered care.*

---

* Imagine if Truman had supported Hill-Aiken, an individually oriented premium support concept. I believe medical care in this country would have followed a very different path, more individualistic and less governmental and far less costly. Perhaps the concept of health savings accounts and high-deductible insurance plans for expensive items might have been conceived decades earlier, and individual Americans would have had the power to choose their physician and hospital care as they saw fit. No question people are more care-

ful spending their own money than everybody else's. As all Americans would have had money for hospital care, there would have been no need for hospitals to be not-for-profit, and they would have to compete regarding both quality and price. Patients spending their own money would develop a closer, longer-lasting relationship with a trusted physician, thereby improving the health care of individuals and of the nation as a whole.

Social Insurance for the Elderly

In 1957 and again in 1959, Congressman Aime Forand (D-RI) submitted a bill to provide medical care to all those over age 65, a form of social insurance. The bill never made it out of the Ways and Means Committee because the committee chairman, Wilbur Mills, (D-AR) had reservations about the scope of the program, its effects on the medical marketplace, and its cost. The bill did raise public awareness of the so-called three-generation family problem, however: middle-aged parents paying their parents' medical bills as well as for their children's education. The junior Senator from Massachusetts, John F. Kennedy, also favored the Forand bill. In response, Congressman Mills and Senator Robert Kerr (D-OK) submitted, Congress passed, and President Eisenhower in 1960 signed the Kerr-Mills Act. It authorized federal support to the states to provide medical care for the elderly poor, which was means-tested. Unfortunately for its supporters, including the AMA, the states did a very poor job of administering the law, with only four states making the full range of medical services available to the elderly poor.[182]

New life for the Forand bill came about with the 1960 election of President John F. Kennedy; it was resurrected in 1961 under the names of Representative Cecil R. King (D-CA) and Senator Clinton P. Anderson (D-NM). The King-Anderson bill originally provided coverage for retirees on Social Security for ninety days of hospitalization and some nursing home care, but no physician payments. Later it was considerably expanded. The AMA rejected the bill, notwithstanding its merits, as the first step in creating a government-dominated medical system, whereby each generation would be supplying benefits to the previous one, including even to those not in need.[183] (The Association did support care for those in need.)*

* Championed by the Federal Security Agency (later Health, Education and Welfare and Health and Human Services) and organized labor, the bill was focused on government involvement, with a heavy bureaucratic presence. The

leaders of the mandatory health insurance movement could see no other way to fund or maintain such a program. The idea of individuals saving for their care throughout a lifetime to be available when elderly, by means of a universal tax credited account was a foreign concept. Up until recently, it has been assumed by almost all policy makers that a continually expanding population would make it possible for succeeding generations to pay for the health care of the previous one. By the 1960s, it should have been obvious that with the population bubble caused by the post–World War II baby boom, this was not going to happen. This demographic fact is now causing significant uncertainty when it comes to funding elderly social programs.

The battle lines were drawn: the AMA against liberal Democrats, the unions, and the federal bureaucracy. Labor helped form the National Council of Senior Citizens for Health Care through Social Security, which held forums throughout the country. The problem for the pro King-Anderson forces was Wilbur Mills, Chairman of Ways and Means in the House; they could not get the bill out of his committee. The Kennedy administration decided on an all-out effort to force the issue. The White House initiated a national campaign that included five thousand speeches given by 250 carefully chosen speakers throughout the country. The finale of this political blitz was a special afternoon event, sponsored by the National Council of Senior Citizens for Health Care through Social Security. President Kennedy spoke at Madison Square Garden; it was broadcast on every TV network, in front of an audience of many thousands of elderly. The AMA fought back with its own campaign of multiple public service announcements, physicians' wives holding coffee klatches, and speeches against government-dominated medicine by an actor, Ronald Reagan.

But how could the AMA respond to a charismatic President speaking to 20,000 cheering seniors that would be watched on all TV networks? The AMA plan was to have their best speaker, Dr. Ed Annis, record his speech to an empty Madison Square Garden just hours after the President's speech. President Kennedy, on his way to the Garden, decided his prepared speech was not adequate and spoke extemporaneously. His speech was generally considered one of the worst, if not *the* worst, of his career; it was later proven that his example of a senior's hardship resulting from a lack of insurance was totally incorrect. Meanwhile, Dr. Annis gave a spellbinding speech against the dramatic backdrop of an empty Madison Square Garden filled with discarded bunting and signs. Dr. Annis's speech was televised to the nation from a recording the next evening on only one network, but with dramatic effect. Not wanting to wait for the November election, President Kennedy forced a vote that passed the House, triggering a vote on July 17, 1962, in the Senate, where King-Anderson lost, 52-48.[184] No one at the time could foresee that a few years later, it would be reconsidered under very different circumstances.[.]

.The leadership of the AMA believed that the defeat of King-Anderson in the Senate was a great victory. But it was a victory from which the organization would never fully recover. Didn't the elderly, typically no longer employed, now have a problem paying for health care, given that most Americans now had employee-based health insurance? And the AMA's favorite law, Kerr-Mills, was not working.

Doctors are supposed to care for people and provide their services to those in need. A government bureaucracy running health care for the elderly in this nation would unquestionably pose serious problems: Costs would greatly escalate as Congressman Mills had feared; the therapeutic bond between patient and doctor would be jeopardized; lobbying to extract as much as possible from the Treasury would become intense; and politicians would become the central actors in American health care. Why not put the money to pay for physicians in individuals' hands and fund hospital insurance? Better yet, have all Americans save money for their health care throughout their lives. None of these ideas came to be official AMA policy, although some members were aware of the AMA's critical lack of foresight.

7

The AMA's Greatest Fear
Government-Controlled Bureaucratic Medicine
Comes to Fruition

Dr. Russell B. Roth, who rose to become President of the AMA in 1973, while serving in the early 1960s as Vice-Chairman of the AMA Council on Medical Service, sent a letter in1962 to the Secretary of the Council on Legislative Activities conveying his concern and displeasure regarding the AMA's lack of a positive stance on insurance for the elderly. He claimed that the association was in a "profound state of auto-hypnosis. . . . By virtue of the togetherness that develops at AMA official sessions, wherein we hear our own lobbyists reporting on their work, listen to the Senators and Representatives we want to hear, and engender in ourselves a collective sense of self-satisfaction and boldness, our top leadership has somehow convinced itself that the AMA is doing just fine. My view is that it is lamentably not doing well at all."[185] Dr. Max H. Parrott, a member of the Council on Legislative Activities, postulated that the 1963–64 House of Delegates (HOD) was divided into three groups regarding health insurance for the elderly: a left-wing element which thought that the AMA should support a government-dominated health care system; a liberal group that wanted an original AMA plan that would provide funding for coverage for all, but within the framework of age-old AMA values of market determination, direct payment of physicians, and absolute patient control over physician choice; and a conservative group, composed of the leadership of the organization, the Board of Trustees, and the Chief Executive Officer, that held sway and championed doing nothing.[186] [187]

Everything changed on November 22, 1963, however, with the assassination of President John F. Kennedy. There immediately arose a groundswell of opinion to follow through on the assassinated President's desire to provide health coverage for elderly Americans. Exactly how this was to be done, the public left up to Washington. Before the 1964 election, with Lyndon Johnson, now President of the United States, leading the way, the King-Anderson Bill, a federally administered plan providing 60 days of hospital/nursing home care for all over 65 but without physician coverage, passed the Senate, 49-44. Wilbur Mills, as

Chairman of the House Ways and Means Committee, was able to stall the bill in the Senate-House Conference Committee, but agreed to bring it up when the new Congress convened. During the election recess, the AMA spent nearly $2 million dollars campaigning against King-Anderson. The AMA favored Kerr-Mills (signed into law by President Eisenhower in 1960), which covered both hospital and physician fees but was means-tested, and was half-heartedly administered by the states as well.[188] In advocating the status quo, the leadership of the AMA failed to understand that circumstances had dramatically changed, and the country wanted a Kennedy-type solution that covered all of the elderly regardless of their financial situation. The AMA thereby lost their last chance to effectively guide federal health policy to a more individualistic approach, rather than a government-centered, heavily bureaucratic plan. After the Democratic landslide of November 1964 and his own election as President, Lyndon Johnson, with a keen sense of Congressional sentiment and a huge Democratic Congressional majority, was ready to push for passage of King-Anderson.[189]

With the new Congress in place, the action was now in the House, with Wilbur Mills the key actor. Calculating that King-Anderson would cover only about 25 percent of the cost of a serious illness, both Mills and the AMA were concerned about an angry backlash.[190] Way too late, after the liberals in the HOD rose to the ascendency, at a special session in early 1965 the AMA developed a plan called "Eldercare." The plan was means-tested and was strongly opposed by Democrats; it cost less, but offered more generous benefits than Kerr-Mills or the eventually passed Medicare. Also proposed by the AMA for the first time was a suggestion of expanding Kerr-Mills to those in need under 65.[191] The AMA spent about $1.5 million publicizing their new plan. The Republicans in Congress, still reeling from the previous November's shellacking at the polls, presented their own plan, submitted by congressman John W. Byrnes (R-WI). This plan would operate on a voluntary basis and covered hospital and physician services for those over 65 through the purchase of private insurance, with federal oversight. Financing was to be two-thirds from general revenues and one-third from pension checks owed to individuals.[192]

Chairman Mills, knowing President Johnson had the committee votes to send a bill to the House for ratification, surprised most in Washington by not supporting any of the three bills—King-Anderson, Eldercare, or Byrnes—but instead combining features of all three.

House bill 6675 had three components: 1) Medicare Part A hospital care, in essence King-Anderson, for Social Security recipients, financed and administered by Social Security; 2) Medicare Part B, essentially the Byrnes Bill, a voluntary insurance plan to augment Part A by covering physician services, financed both by premiums from those electing participation and by general federal revenues; and 3) Medicaid, patterned after the AMA's proposal to provide care for the indigent under age 65, funded by both federal and state monies and administered by the states. This House bill was sent to the Senate; the AMA testified against it, disagreeing with federal administration and management of any part of these plans. The AMA warned that given open-ended benefits and patients divorced from any knowledge of fees, with time the costs of these programs would become untenable; in addition, millions of dollars of free physician services would now be assumed by the government.[193] But with presidential support and under Wilbur Mills's careful watch, his plan passed the House, the Senate concurred, and Title 18, Medicare, and Title 19, Medicaid, became amendments to the Social Security Act. President Johnson signed the law on July 31, 1965 in Independence, Missouri, to honor Harry S. Truman.

Wanting the AMA to have some impact on forthcoming Medicare/Medicaid legislation, Dr. Russell Roth suggested at the June 1965 HOD meeting that the leadership have the authority to meet with the executive to have some influence over writing the law's regulations. The HOD also gave the leadership the authority to meet with the President to ensure continuance of the highest quality of care for the American people. For a pro like Lyndon Johnson, these meetings were wonderful theater, in which he emphasized his tremendous respect for physicians and could tell AMA representatives that he welcomed their help in formulating the regulations.[194] Further meetings with the President took place in which he supported the AMA's concerns on impending legislation regarding referral patterns; and the President made sure that there was ample AMA representation on many Medicare/Medicaid advisory panels.[195] In effect, President Johnson was able to convince the AMA leadership to "bury the hatchet", work with the government, which the AMA had previously sworn not to do, and become a willing participant in government bureaucracy–dominated and –controlled medicine.

Rank-and-file AMA members called for a special HOD meeting in Chicago in October 1965, feeling frustration and anger toward the leadership. But in the end they realized that there was no choice: they had to participate for the sake of their patients and deliver the best care possible.*

> * It is doubtful if many at that meeting realized that the real problem was that over forty-five years, the AMA had been unable to preempt government control over medicine by its failure to propose substitute measures. It had taken years for the AMA to support private, employer-based insurance—and that had left the unemployed and retired Americans uninsured. Kerr-Mills was a lame duck. Free care by physicians was laudable but left gaps in care, especially by hospitals. Taxpayer funding of medical research was rapidly increasing physicians' armamentarium; and since this research was funded on the national level, it only stood to reason that all citizens should benefit. John Kennedy's assassination and Lyndon Johnson's landslide 1964 victory set the stage for Medicare/Medicaid. In the absence of any creative measures proposed by the AMA to ensure care for all Americans, government-controlled medicine was inevitable.

Bastiat's Laws of Unintended Consequences[196]

Frédéric Bastiat (1801–50), an economist and follower of Adam Smith and member of the French Assembly, was concerned about the unintended consequences of political action. These quotes represent some of his thinking.

"In the economic sphere an act, a habit, an institution, a law produces not only one effect, but a series of effects. Of these effects, the first alone is immediate; it appears simultaneously with its cause; it is seen. The other effects emerge only subsequently; they are not seen; we are fortunate if we foresee them."

"There is only one difference between a bad economist and a good one: the bad economist confines himself to the visible effect; the good economist takes into account both the effect that can be seen and those effects that must be foreseen."

"Yet this difference is tremendous; for it almost always happens that when the immediate consequence is favorable, the latter consequences are disastrous, and vice versa. Whence it follows that the bad economist pursues a small present good that will be followed by a great evil to come, while the good economist pursues a great good to come, at risk of a small present evil."

The Unintended Consequences
of Medicare and Medicaid

Almost immediately after the passing of Medicare and Medicaid, the volume of hospital utilization increased dramatically, though no provision had been made to offset demand with supply. Hospital admissions increased by 25 percent, surgical procedures by 40 percent, and hospital days by 50 percent.[197] The increase in accessibility to medical care was laudable, but the increase in costs had been drastically underestimated: The House Ways and Means Committee projected hospital costs that were about one-fourth of the actual amount. Research demonstrated that in areas in which seniors' cost sharing (co-pays or deductibles) was lowest, hospital care costs had increased the most.[198] At the same time as Medicare was paying physicians according to the imprecise criterion of "usual, customary, and reasonable," physician Medicare payments increased at an accelerated rate.[199] Unforeseen was the phenomenal growth and expense of maintaining the non-physician workforce needed to operate this government-centered, increasingly complex program, as seen in *Figure 1*.

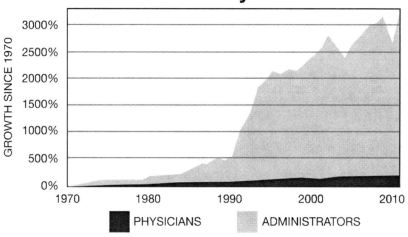

Figure 1:
Additional Source – "High Cost Impact of More Regulations and Staff on Health Care Inflation", Frank Hill, Family Security Matters.org, July 27, 2012

In response to escalating hospital costs, in 1983, Medicare entered the price-fixing world, with the attendant distortion of pricing, by establishing diagnostic-related groups (DRG) for hospital payments. First used as an industrial management tool, DRG was adopted for Medicare after first being applied to hospital payments in New Jersey. Since its inception, multiple changes have been made to DRG with modifiers reflecting the severity of illness and type of hospital. Originally intended only for Medicare patients, the system has been adopted in various forms for non-Medicare patients, but with different negotiated rates.[200] Because Medicare DRG rates pay hospitals approximately 20 percent less than private insurance, frequently below cost, monies are then made up by increased premiums born by those under age 65.[201] Major hospitals such as the Mayo Clinic have incurred substantial losses from DRG payments: in 2008, Mayo lost $840 million while collecting $1.7 billion treating Medicare patients.[202]

To make up for these losses, Mayo, like all hospitals, needs to collect considerable sums in excess of costs from private insurers. Such billing practices illustrate an important point: private insurers are to a considerable extent subsidizing Medicare—and, to an even greater extent because of its lower reimbursement rates, Medicaid. Private insurance premiums must increase to cover these costs, and they are borne by the working population—in essence, a hidden tax funding these federal programs. These increases in insurance premiums are in part responsible for workers' take-home pay in real dollars having remained stagnant over the past decade.[203] Of necessity, hospitals have become quite adroit at working with insurance companies to maximize their income from privately insured patients while at the same time maintaining their not-for-profit status.

One method of doing so is to minimize transparency so as to maximize apparent prices beyond any sense of reason. The scorpion bite story of Phoenix, Arizona, is illustrative of the absurdity of hospital pricing owing to the lack of market discipline.[204] A patient bitten by a scorpion was properly admitted and treated with anti-venom—which costs $100/dose when it is manufactured in Mexico, but $3,250/dose when made in the U.S., in large part because of the required costly studies needed to obtain FDA approval. The hospital administered two doses and charged the patient $80,000, along with $3,000 for the room and other expenses. Insurance paid $57,000, and the hospital asked the patient to pay the balance because of its "apparent loss." That "loss" helped the hospital maintain its not-for-profit status. The insurance company claims a savings from the employer's insurance plan of $26,000, of which it receives a percentage. The huge variability of hospital charges as each institution has evolved such elaborate solutions for dealing with its Medicare/Medicaid losses has recently received a fair amount of press.[205]

Medicare/Medicaid, then, has created a situation wherein both hospitals and the insurance industry have ventured into nefarious financial manipulations. As hospital care consumes the largest portion of our nation's health care dollars (as shown in *Figure 2*), such perverse financial arrangements have distorted the pricing of our entire health care industry. With Washington as the center of the health care price-fixing scheme, creative lobbying by special interests has made it possible to divert significant amounts of the nation's resources *to* those interests.[*][206]

U.S. health care spending breakdown, 2010

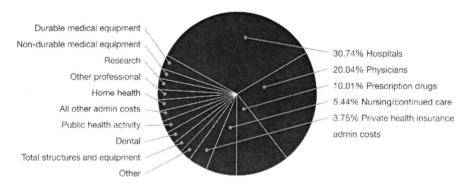

Figure 2:
U.S. health care spending breakdown, 2010. Source: Center for Medicare and Medicaid Services.

[*] The solution is requiring complete pricing transparency, and imposing the discipline of market forces on both hospitals and insurance companies. This has been pioneered by the Surgery Center of Oklahoma; see http://www.surgerycenterok.com/.

This subtle inter-generational theft from the succeeding generation, has many difficulties. We have also burdened them with a huge national debt, but for many we are not providing adequate education to be able to compete in a world wide industrial economy.

Being a price-fixed system, Medicare pays all hospitals the same base rate, adjusting by applying a complicated formula that accounts for regional variation in the area wage index.[207] This means that community and university teaching hospitals are paid the same for each DRG code. But these two types of hospitals should serve our society in different and distinct ways and as such should have different pricing. Community hospitals should excel at delivering standardized care more efficiently; thus their costs should be somewhat less. University hospitals should be delivering new cutting-edge medicine along with teaching and research, with higher attendant costs deserving a price differential. Because this is impossible under the present system, we are now witnessing a blurring of this distinction. Many community hospitals now offer procedures that used to be performed only at university medical centers. University academic medical centers, for their part, are pursuing more patient care to cover costs, in many instances delivering care that used to be the purview of community hospitals. This change in focus for many is diminishing the traditional university medical centers' mission of research, teaching, and the development of cutting-edge medicine. University hospitals are asking their physicians to see more patients, thereby detracting from their teaching and research activities. As predicted by Nobel Prize–winning economist Milton Freidman, they, along with some community hospitals, are now facing serious financial concerns owing to the government's need to conserve funds and the academic centers' huge fixed costs.[208] Especially in light of shrinking National Institutes of Health funding in inflation-adjusted dollars, most university hospitals are devoting fundraising to building state-of-the-art clinical facilities as they compete for paying patients. Ideally their fundraising capabilities should be used to further endow their original academic mission.*[209] As a result, the nature of the composition of the typical medical center's faculty is changing as well. This change in emphasis, along with trainees spending less time with patients and more with electronic medical records, puts America's position as the premier nation for the teaching and development of advanced medicine at risk.[210]

* Some real increase in NIH funding has recently come about as a result of 21st Century Cures. http://bit.ly/1lTfwfU

"Curst greed of gold, what crimes thy tyrant power has caused"
(Publius Vergilius Maro, a.k.a. Virgil, 70-19 B.C.E.)

There is a huge imbalance between what an individual pays into Medicare and the cost of the services she or he receives. On average, each

Medicare patient receives about two to three times in cost of services what each paid into the system. Without significant changes, this imbalance is projected to increase.[211] As these costs are made up by the succeeding generation, this amounts to a massive transfer of wealth from the younger to the older generation. If, as this imbalance was developing, Congress had increased Medicare taxes to offset the cost, taxpayer pushback might have resulted in significant changes in the program. This has not happened, and as a result many seniors are pleased to receive these extended benefits. They are reluctant to accept any changes in Medicare that might in essence diminish this free ride.

Supporters of government-dominated health care invoke the supposed lower percentage of Medicare administrative costs, as opposed to those associated with private insurance, 3 percent versus 15-20 percent, to defend their position.[212] There are multiple reasons why this is a misleading argument, however. Since 1977, with the creation of the Health Care Financing Administration (HCFA), Medicare and Medicaid were separated from Social Security and were made responsible for health programs.[213] As other federal agencies—the Internal Revenue Service, the Social Security Administration, Health and Human Services—perform administrative tasks for HCFA, many of its administrative costs are hidden.[214] HCFA does not pay state taxes while private insurers do, adding to the latter's administrative costs. But the largest factor in the deception is the dollars spent on the insured, which is the denominator in calculating the percentage spent on administration. Since Medicare covers those over 65, their medical expenses are much higher, so the percentage spent on administrative costs is lower. The only fair way to compare the two is *administrative costs per patient*. As can be seen in *Figure 3*, in 2005, private insurer administrative costs per patient were $453 while Medicare's costs, despite all of its advantages, were $509.

Two demographic factors, not accounted for at the creation of Medicare, have severely threatened its long-term financial viability.[215] There were 4 workers per retiree in 1965; there are 3.4 now and there will be an expected 2.3 in 2030. Additionally, as a result of improved medical care, average life expectancy in the U.S. has increased from 70.2 years in 1965 to 78.4 in 2010. These two factors have resulted in fewer individuals subsidizing the increased health care costs of the elderly, as they live longer and carry a greater disease burden. Thus the succeeding generation is experiencing an ever-increasing financial burden.

Outlays per Benificiary:
Medicare vs. Private Insurance

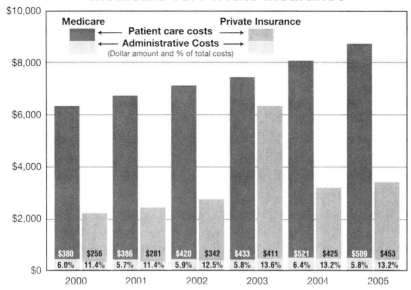

Figure 3:
Source – Robert A. Book, WebMemo. The Heritage Foundation, "Medicare Administrative Costs Are Higher, Not Lower, Than For Private Insurance," No.2505 June 25, 2009

The escalating costs of Medicare and Medicaid have dramatically outpaced the growth of our overall economy. In 1990 the actual federal cost of the programs was $110 billion, in 2000 the cost was $219 billion, and in 2010, $520 billion—and the projected cost in 2020 is $1 trillion.[216] Unlike Social Security, which has a set payment schedule, Medicare/Medicaid have no limit on expenditures per patient.[217] In 1960, before Medicare/Medicaid, individuals paid 52 percent of the nation's health expenditures out of pocket; by 2008 that had decreased to 12 percent. With Medicare supplemental insurance now carried by about 90 percent of Medicare patients, and given the non-transparency of real prices and the open-endedness of the benefit, there is little individual concern regarding expense, and hence the explosion in cost.

The Creation of Resource-Based Relative Value Scale and CPT Codes in an Attempt to Control Costs

Desperate to control escalating Medicare/Medicaid costs, the federal government introduced another price-fixing scheme, this time one for physicians. The Center for Medicare/Medicaid services funded a study led by William Hsiao of the Harvard School of Public Health in 1988, which they used to create the "Resource Based Relative Value Scale" (RBRVS) in 1992.[218] This reimbursement system attempts to assign the relative worth of a physician's services by quantifying three components: the physician's work, the expense of the practice, and the cost of professional liability insurance. It is totally devoid of any market parameters of quality or price; there is no adjustment for the demand for a particular medical service or for the expertise of the physician. Every conceivable physician service is assigned a Current Procedural Terminology—a CPT code. The AMA develops the CPT codes, with an assigned value made up of the three components used to determine a Relative Value Unit (RVU). This RVU is then multiplied by a conversion factor to generate the payment amount for that service. The complexity of the conversion factor includes an adjustment for regional cost-of-living differences.

As a new physician service develops, a new CPT code is created. An AMA committee, the Relative Value Update Committee (RUC), which in effect determines physician incomes, then determines its relative value. Newer codes are funded by subtracting value from older codes. RVUs must by law be reevaluated every five years, using detailed survey data from the physicians involved. Another term, the GPCI (the geographic practice cost index), was introduced to account for local cost-of-living differences. The calculation for each individual payment is: (work RVU x work GPCI) + (practice expense RVU x GPCI) + (malpractice RVU x GPCI) = Total RVU x conversion factor = Medicare payment. Medicare and almost all private insurers reimburse physicians for their services based on this price-fixing payment scheme.[219]

The deliberations of the RUC are secret and highly political, with the largest reimbursements going to the specialties with the greatest clout.[220] The folly of this highly political price control scheme that has been in effect for the past twenty-two years is well described in an essay by Phillips Gausewitz.[221] With the inception of the Resource Based Relative Value Scale in 1992, there has been no market determination of the cost of any physician service covered by Medicare. Those services not included under this scheme—e. g., Lasik surgery—have undergone large decreases in price and increases in quality.[222] With no market discipline determining value, it is unknown if some physician services would otherwise cost less, and others more.

Congress has given the AMA the exclusive right to sell the CPT code books needed for billing, creating a monopoly resulting in millions of dollars in income.[223] For the AMA this could be described as an example of bidirectional "regulatory capture." The AMA benefits by bringing in a great deal of money and maintaining its image as a central player in the federal government's heavily bureaucratic role in health care. Congress gains leverage over the AMA by threatening elimination of the monopoly should the AMA not go along with Congressional will. In the long run this is not in the best interests of the nation, as physician input with respect to various Congressional proposals must be circumspect in order not to lose its cash cow.

The price-fixed bureaucratic billing system is continuously increasing in complexity and cost as the ever-expanding International Classification of Diseases (ICD) diagnostic codes have to be integrated with the physician CPT codes to create billing documents.[224] It is obvious that despite the Medicare RBRVS, its attempts at cost control have failed, and will continue to do so without significant change.[*]

[*] The current billing system, which employs many thousands of ancillary personnel (see figure 1), would be far less complex and much more representative of reality if price transparency and market-determined reimbursements replaced arbitrarily assigned payment schedules. And the present highly bureaucratic, government-centered billing system is siphoning considerable resources away from direct patient care.

The Growth and Path of Medicaid

When created in 1965 as part of Wilbur Mills's legislative package, Medicaid was viewed as a combined federal-state welfare program, with funding shared between the federal government and the individual states. On average the federal government pays for 57 percent of Medicaid's costs, with variations depending on the state's per capita income. The stimulus package of 2009 temporarily increased the federal share of Medicaid expenditures to 64 percent until this feature's expiration in 2011. The effects of the Affordable Care Act on Medicaid are hard to predict with precision, as enrollment fluctuates considerably with the state of the economy, but ultimately the ACA is expected to substantially expand the program.[225]

Initially those receiving Medicare were called "beneficiaries," while those receiving Medicaid were called "recipients."[226] This changed in

1996 when Medicaid was de-linked from welfare in accordance with the Personal Responsibility and Work Opportunity Reconciliation Act, with Medicaid patients now also being called "beneficiaries."[227] Thus Medicaid went from a welfare program to an insurance program—one that has seen very significant growth over the years. In 1966, Medicaid served 4 million Americans; in 2014, 65 million—a 1,525 percent increase[228]— while the U.S. population went from an estimated 195,501,000 in 1966 to 313,914,040 in 2012, a 60.5 percent increase.[229] In 2002, Medicaid became the largest insurance program in the country, public or private.[230]

Medicaid eligibility guidelines and therefore expenditures are quite complex and can vary from state to state.*[231] In 1966 the cost of Medicaid was $0.5 billion for the federal government and $0.4 billion for state governments, totaling $0.9 billion. In 2014 the cost for the federal government is expected to be $304.4 billion and for state governments $203.6 billion, for a total of $508.0 billion.[232] Without significant changes in the program, the projected cost in 2020 will be a total of $752.8 billion: $451.4 billion for the federal government and $301.4 billion for state governments.[233] Although inflation does affect these dollar amounts, a dollar in 1966 was worth $7.33 in 2014[234], while the increase in Medicaid expenditures from 1966 to 2014 was 564.4-fold.

> * Perhaps Congress would have paused before enacting Medicaid if they could have foreseen an over thousand- fold increase in the Medicaid population. The Affordable Care Act has added additional millions to the Medicaid rolls. This number of Medicaid-eligible patients reflects that our nation has yet to successfully deal with poverty despite spending trillions of dollars. Someday we will hopefully gain the wisdom to use these trillions to learn how to free succeeding generations from the shackles of poverty.

Does spending this vast amount of resources to provide health care for the poor, for children, for pregnant women, and for nursing home residents, among others, provide ready access to care? For many if not most Medicaid recipients unfortunately not, because Medicaid pays about 72 percent of the Medicare payment schedule, which in turn is significantly less than private insurance, causing physicians and hospitals to lose considerable amounts while treating each Medicaid patient.[235]

The unintended consequence of Medicaid's basic design is that the federal government does not determine reimbursement rates to physicians and hospitals; those payments are determined by the states. The Secretary of Health and Human Services does have statutory authority to suspend the federal government's share of payments to the states, should it be determined that provider payments are not "sufficient to enlist enough providers so that care and services are available under the plan at least to the extent that such care and services are available to the general population in the geographic area."[236] In reality the Secretary cannot exercise this authority, however, because those who would suffer the most under a suspension of federal payments would be the very population that the law is intended to help! It would not be difficult for any state's Congressional delegation to muster support from other states to punish HHS should the Secretary decide to withhold payment. There had been the possibility of judicial review, especially on account of the Boron amendment, by which states determine reimbursement rates that are "reasonable and adequate"; but Congress repealed the amendment under pressure from the states in 1997.[237] In January 2012 the U.S. Supreme Court scheduled the case of *Douglas v. Independent Living Center of Southern California et al.* along with two other consolidated cases involving lawsuits against the state of California for reducing Medicaid reimbursement rates in 2008. While the case was pending, however, the Centers for Medicare & Medicaid Services found the reductions acceptable and consequently the court did not decide the case, instead vacating the Ninth Circuit of Appeals finding and sending the case back to the lower courts in effect negating the suit.[238]

The Affordable Care Act, while it expands Medicaid eligibility, does not address the states' authority to assign payment rates.*[239] Furthermore, in order to help ensure funding for the ACA, Medicare's physician and hospital reimbursement will be below Medicaid rates by the year 2020 without changes in the law.[240] Unless there are significant changes in the structure of these two federal programs, access issues for their beneficiaries will in all likelihood become a major problem.

* In reality, it is extremely unlikely, given a deficit-ridden federal government and tight budgets affecting state governments, that there will be significant improvement in Medicaid payment rates in the foreseeable future.

Effectiveness of Medicaid

Does giving patients Medicaid insurance decrease their subsequent resort to the Emergency Room? The longest experience is in Massachusetts, where the results are quite clear: emergency room visits actually *increased* after the initiation of their state health care reform. Summarizing an article from the *Annals of Emergency Medicine*, records from sixty-nine Massachusetts hospitals experiencing about 2 million ER visits annually were studied between 2004, two years before reform, to 2009, two years after the full effect of reform. Medicaid patients accounted for the largest increase in visits: 23.6 percent before versus 29.7 percent after Medicaid expansion. The authors of the article note that, "[t]his study should further weaken the long-held notion that high use of the emergency department is being driven mainly by the uninsured."[241]

A larger increase in ER use by Medicaid patients was also recently observed in Oregon.[242] In 2008, Oregon initiated a limited expansion of Medicaid by lottery. This created an opportunity to study in a controlled manner those who received Medicaid versus those who did not. Emergency room visits by 25,000 new Medicaid patients in the Portland area were compared with those from an equal number of those not receiving Medicaid over an eighteen-month period. Those on Medicaid made 40 percent more visits than those who did not—and many of these increased visits were on account of issues that could have been treated by a primary care physician. The records of this same group of Medicaid-insured patients versus those without insurance were also studied for medical outcomes.[243] The positives were: those with Medicaid had a decreased probability of a positive screening for depression; there was increased use of preventative services; large out-of-pocket expenses were eliminated; diagnoses of diabetes increased, as did medication use. But there were important negatives as well: no significant improvement in diabetes control; and high blood pressure and elevated cholesterol levels when present were unchanged, as were the medications prescribed for their treatment when comparing the Medicaid insured versus the uninsured.[244]

Another study compared the results of surgery performed on patients with private insurance versus those with Medicaid in fifty-two Michigan hospitals from July 2012 to June 2013.[245] Though the Medicaid patients were on average younger, they had significantly more postoperative complications and twice as high mortality. Medicaid patients also had greater lengths of stay and a higher likelihood of readmission. Similar results were found in an earlier University of Virginia study.[246] Correcting for confounding factors (age, other morbidities, nutritional status, etc.), the University of Virginia researchers studied the outcomes of 893,658 major surgical operations from a nationwide database from 2003 to 2007. They found that Medicaid patients had almost twice the in-hospital death rate as those with private insurance, stayed 42 percent longer, and cost 26 percent more. Compared with those with no insurance, Medicaid patients were 13 percent more likely to die, had 50 percent longer hospital stays, and cost 20 percent more. The reasons for these adverse results are unclear, but may represent overall socio-economic status. There are studies by economists showing that Medicaid patients do better, but their methodology is open to serious criticism.[247]

An Alternative: Better Care, Less Cost

There is an example in the United States where a different Medicaid program was created so that patients could receive care on a par with those with private insurance at significantly lower cost.[248] Indiana gained a waiver from the federal government to use money from a cigarette tax to expand Medicaid to an additional 45,000 citizens. Unlike those covered under standard Medicaid, this group was given a bank account, called a power account, and a high-deductible health insurance plan (HDHP). Participants were required to contribute their own money (2–5 percent of their income, up to a maximum of $92.00/month) to remain in the program; families earning 0-100 percent of the Federal Poverty Level contributed 2 percent of their income to their account monthly.[249] The state contributed $1,100 into the account yearly, which equaled the deductible for the insurance policy; there were no other patient requirements (such as deductibles) for care. They were able to seek physician care of their choice, using their power account money; this money was available only for health care. Money left in the account each year could be used toward their contribution for the following year if they had obtained an annual physical, pap smears and mammograms where appropriate, cholesterol screening, flu vaccination, blood glucose screening, and screens for immunity to tetanus and diphtheria. To avoid employers canceling their coverage for their lowest-paid employees, one had to be unemployed for six months to be eligible.

The program has been wildly successful. Poor people wisely managed their power account money and their own care, with a 98 percent participants' approval rating. Preventative care increased, emergency room visits decreased, and costs per patient significantly decreased.[250] Avik Roy has calculated that we as a nation could replicate the success of the Indiana plan for about 40 percent less than what we are now spending.[251] His plan would have all Medicaid patients directly contract with a physician, such as those with Epiphany Health.[252] For an individual the cost is about $80.00/month or $960.00/year plus $2,500 for a high-deductible health plan in the patient's name, for a total of $3,460/year. The cost for a family is modestly higher. Epiphany has also demonstrated that laboratory and x-ray tests cost much less when paid for in cash. These monies could be paid into Medicaid beneficiaries' health savings accounts, from which all expenses would be paid. They would be able to direct their own care at far less cost and with far better results than at the present time.

The unintended consequences of the 1965 Medicare/Medicaid legislation are myriad. People are much more careful spending money they perceive as their own than they are with everybody else's tax dollars. From mine and others' experience, the relationship between patient and doctor is more intense, personal, and meaningful as well as more cost-conscious when patients spend their own money. The experiences of Indiana, Singapore, and Switzerland readily demonstrate that patients obtain excellent care at far less cost under such an arrangement than with the government-centered, highly bureaucratic system that now exists in the U.S.

Under the current system, the burden on the succeeding generation funding Medicare is excessive and unnecessary. If all Americans were accumulating funds (via their present payroll deduction), for their health care in a special account with a conservative investment policy throughout their lifetime, for most of the population there would be more than adequate funds for their care when elderly. Then when elderly this account could be merged with their pre-existing own health savings account (HSA). Each individual's HSA would have to be accompanied with a high-deductible health plan (HDHP) for big-ticket items. For those, about 10 percent of the population, who develop a chronic disease before the age of 65, reinsurance funds would have to be available to augment their HSA and HDHP. The reinsurance funds could be financed by an actuarially derived surtax on the premium paid for their HDHP. This would solve the problem of "pre-existing conditions" as the 1996 HIPPA legislation prohibits the cancelling of an existing policy due to the advent of disease. Complete price transparency would be required, and with all Americans able to pay for their health care, hospitals would no longer have a need to be not-for-profit and participate in extensive price gaming. We do not have to be chained to a system of health care initiated in the nineteenth century that is impersonal and excessively expensive, and leaves many with poor outcomes.

8

THE ILL-FATED 1997 MEDICARE PHYSICIAN PAYMENT ADJUSTMENT, THE SUSTAINABLE GROWTH RATE (SGR) – AND ITS REPLACEMENT, THE MEDICARE ACCESS AND CHIP REAUTHORIZATION ACT (MACRA) – FUTILITY IN ACTION

Introduction

In most transactions when consumers purchase services the fees are agreed upon in large part depending on market forces. But with Medicare as it is now configured, patients have little to no responsibility, nor knowledge of the costs of their transactions. Physicians, for their part, are paid according to a price-fixed schedule created in Washington that ignores demand, expertise, experience, and skills. Although this arrangement is referred to as "fee for service," this is a misnomer, as the government pays the physician an arbitrary fee while the individual receiving the service has no knowledge of that fee. Just as hospitals and insurance companies have manipulated hospital costs, creating a bizarre pricing system, the price-fixed physician payment scheme has also created distortions in behavior. Trying in vain to deal with escalating Medicare costs, Congress attempts ever more complex methods of adjusting its price-fixed methodology. The Sustainable Growth Rate (SGR) was an example of a government's desperate attempt to control costs, in this case as it pertains to physician reimbursement.[253] It created a law impossible to implement while creating a huge yearly distraction. The law was recently abandoned at even more cost while imposing a greater bureaucratic burden on physicians detracting from patient care. The SGR "fix", the Medicare Access and CHIP Reauthorization Act (MACRA) tries to do the impossible: evaluating quality via computer algorithms for 40 trillion transactions per year using imprecise data. These dubious calculations then penalize or reward physicians via decreased or increased payments. Physician pushback has been intense.[*254]

---

* While being repeatedly warned that Medicare is presently unsustainable, our government continues to pursue the present centralized, increasingly complex and expensive price-fixed system while progressively destroying the patient-physician relationship.

The SGR

Recall from Chapter 7 the formula for physician reimbursement in the price-fixed system of the Resource Based Relative Value Scale: (work RVU x GPCI) + (practice expense RVU x GPCI) + (malpractice RVU x GPCI) = Total RVU x conversion Factor = Medicare payment. This chapter discusses the multiplier, the *conversion factor*. But first some definitions[255]:

1) *Relative Value Units (RVUs) — a means of defining the value of a physician's service without reference to the discipline of the market, by estimating technical skill, mental and physical effort, judgment, and psychological stress, along with practice expense and medical liability insurance costs. These estimates are on the basis of CPT codes.*

2) *Geographic Practice Cost Indices (GPCI) — reflects geographic differences in the cost of living, some practice expenses, and the cost of professional liability insurance.*

3) *The Medicare Economic Index (MEI) — an inflationary factor calculated on the basis of changes in hourly earnings in the general economy; expenses for operating an office; the cost of medical materials, supplies, and equipment; and employee fringe benefits.*

4) *The expenditure target adjustment — reflecting a comparison between actual Medicare physician spending and the growth in the overall economy*

Converting RVUs to actual payments requires the calculation of a *conversion factor*. Previously the *conversion factor* was calculated using the MEI, an expenditure target adjustment, and adjustments reflecting new legislation or intended to achieve budget neutrality. From January 1992 (the inception of the Resource Based Relative Value Scale) until passage of the Balanced Budget Act in August 1997, the *conversion factor*, using the above four parameters, was calculated by a formula called the Medicare Volume Performance Standard (MVPS). Even before the MVPS was instituted, however, a report issued by Bernardin and Schoenman (Project HOPE Center for Health Affairs) in 1991 advised that this mechanism was not adequate "for addressing problems [of] inappropriate utilization and access."[256] And, as reported by Senator

Max Baucus (D-MT), the MVPS "was not very effective in limiting total professional expenditures."*257

* Price-fixing mechanisms have failed throughout world history—and in the United States, during the Nixon administration. But once a paradigm has been established, especially given a body such as the U.S. Congress along with interested lobbying parties, it becomes extremely difficult to admit a mistake and choose a different path. It is therefore not surprising that Congress in its ongoing effort to control Medicare costs tried merely to adjust the conversion factor, on the basis of another, more complex formula.

As part of the Balanced Budget Act of 1997, Congress settled on another plan, the Sustainable Growth Rate (SGR) to calculate the *conversion factor*, attempting to control growth in aggregate Medicare physician costs. The SGR was calculated using four parameters: 1) the estimated percentage change in physician fees for services, 2) the estimated percentage changes in Medicare fee-for-service enrollment, 3) the estimated percentage growth in real per capita gross domestic product on a ten-year rolling average, and 4) the estimated percentage changes in spending owing to changes in law and regulation.[258]

From the Centers for Medicare & Medicaid Services, Office of the Actuary, April 2013: "The CY 2014 physician fee schedule update is determined according to a statutory formula by multiplying (i) one plus the percentage change in the Medicare Economic Index (MEI), and (ii) one plus the update adjustment factor (UAF), and then subtracting one. . . . The UAF compares actual and target expenditures, and, for a given year, is determined by a formula, as shown below:

> *UAF2014 = Target2013 – Actual2013/Actual2013× 0.75 +*
>
> *{Target4/96-12/13 – Actual4/96-12/13/Actual2013 × (1 + SGR2014)} × 0.33. . . . Using this information, the estimated CY 2014 Conversion Factor is determined by applying the CY 2014 MEI and the CY 2014 UAF to the CY 2013 conversion factor that would have applied for CY 2013 (the CY 2013 pre-legislation conversion fac-tor). The estimated CY 2014 Conversion Factor update of –24.4 percent is calculated by dividing the estimated CY 2014 conversion factor by the CY 2013 conversion factor and subtracting 1."[259]*

* It appears that logic on this point is lost on the Congress. No matter how complex the formula, no matter how large the bureaucracy and the expense to accumulate the necessary data can this process work? If Congress indeed has a fear that decreasing physician reimbursement will jeopardize access for Medicare patients, can any formula, no matter how complex, calculate decreasing physician payments in a way that will not imperil such access?

The Balanced Budget Act was written in such a way that if Congress delayed calculated decreases in physician payments in a given year, these decreases would aggregate, so that over time this would create a prohibitively large percentage decrease in payments. Note in the quotation from Mr. Clemens of the Department of Health and Human Services (see above) that the calculated decrease for 2014 if Congress had not interceded would be greater than 20 percent. That is because since 2002, Congress, usually late in the year and usually in the midst of howling from medical societies, has postponed any decrease for the past twelve years.

The year 2014 was to be different: A "fix" to this yearly crisis requiring Congressional action was thought to be a "sure thing." The American College of Physicians published an essay summarizing the various Congressional committees' actions to repeal the SGR and replace it with other refinements to this price-fixed payment scheme. Congress got to the point of having a House and Senate Conference Committee discuss H.R. 4015/S. 2000, the SGR Repeal and Medicare Provider Payment Modernization Act of 2014—comprehensive legislation to repeal the Sustainable Growth Rate and move toward a "value-based" payment and delivery system.*

* How does a bureaucracy instead of an individual patient decide value, when neither the patient nor the doctor knows the real market value of the service being rendered? More computer-based hoops for the physician to go through to determine value are flawed. Thus, MACRA supposedly replacing value for volume is at best sophomoric, as it is impossible to determine value in a price-fixed system.

The report reveals how organized medicine sees the federal government, not the patient, as in charge of physician payment: In essence the government is the client, while the patient is an excuse to render a bill. ACP has long-advocated that the flawed SGR formula needs to be repealed and replaced with positive, predictable and permanent payment updates.[260] The American College of Physicians also published their reasons for supporting this legislation; it would, they advised:

1) *End the SGR cuts forever.*

2) *Add $140 billion to physician pay over the next 10 years.*

3) *Cancel the 2016 PQRS (Physician Quality Reporting System – part of the HITECH Act) meaningful use penalties.*

4) *Provide a 5% bonus to physicians in new alternative payment models, such as PCMHs (Patient Centered Medical Homes) and ACOs (Accountable Care Organizations).**

---

* PCMH is the bureaucracy attempting to duplicate the good old-fashioned patient-doctor relationship; let patients pay the doctor directly out of their tax credited health account. ACOs have led to huge hospital consolidation, decreasing competition.

5) *Create options for physicians to earn positive updates for participating in a new value-based payment program.*

6) *Combine and harmonize the existing Medicare PQRS, meaningful use, and Medicare value modifier index into a single VBP reporting program.*

7) *Establish a process to improve the accuracy of relative value units (RVUs).*

8) *Provide funding to help smaller practices successfully participate in the new value-based payment program or in alternative payment models.*

9) *Increase federal funding for development of quality measures.*

10) *[Help] ensure that Medicare patients will continue to have access to physicians, the most of all the changes it makes from current law.**[261]

---

* It is difficult to discern if either party, members of Congress or the medical societies, really believed that any of these good things would be possible, with make-believe prices and given that an overwhelming bureaucracy would be necessary to accomplish any of these goals. It is worrisome that Congress would be willing to spend considerable sums of money, much of it borrowed, and commit millions of physician man-hours on schemes without trials testing efficacy. There is no doubt in my mind that if Congress members were spending their own money and time, they would insist on proof-of-concept before large-scale funding of this or any other scheme.

In the end, the whole package fell apart, with Congress unable to find the more than $100 billion necessary to make up for the lost dollars if the SGR were in fact repealed. Congress again passed a postponement of the 20+ percent decrease in physician payments, which was signed by the President. This lost opportunity to "fix" the SGR was the subject of an essay by Stuart Guterman in the *New England Journal of Medicine*. He rightly pointed out that the SGR does not, in the present third-party-dominated payment system, address the problems of excess volume, intensity of services, or the quality, appropriateness, or coordination of care. The idea that an individual patient spending his or her own money, possibly from a health savings account, would be more efficient than a distant bureaucracy in controlling these shortcomings was not addressed. Guterman comments that the SGR, which imposes cuts in payments to all physicians, punishes those who are practicing efficient cost-control medicine. He demonstrates that spending per beneficiary has increased independently of variations in Medicare physician payment rates, and he looks forward to third-party payment methods that achieve the laudable goals of better, more efficient care.*[262]

---

* Since its inception in 1965, Medicare has relied on a third-party payment system; almost all interested entities—government, academics, physician groups, hospital associations, the pharmaceutical industry, and the device industry, among others—have a difficult time imagining alternative, patient-centered compensation.

There are many reasons why medical societies should not pursue increased reimbursements from the federal government, instead of seeking a system whereby market values determine physician payment. Among them:

1) *In the eyes of the public, it makes physicians look greedy.*

2) *It puts politicians in charge of a patient's care.*

3) *As much of the federal money is borrowed, in essence our grandchildren are liable for a good portion of these increases, with interest.*

4) *It allows lobbying pressures to distort the payment system for their own gain.*

5) *It encourages the federal government to impose ever-increasing and burdensome reporting methods to justify payment, which diverts attention from patient care.*

It would seem reasonable that after repeated failures, including the SGR, in trying to control Medicare physician costs without limiting patient access, Congress and the public would try a different course: to think of ways to put the individual patient in charge of the money, instead of trying and failing to control costs in a heavily bureaucratic, government-centered way. This works in other countries, such as Switzerland and Singapore. Additionally, we must find ways so that, with time, those still working will not be burdened with the costs of health care for the previous generation.

Alas, April 2015 saw the end of SGR; it was called, "A great bipartisan victory." The bill is titled, the Medicare Access and CHIP Reauthorization Act (MACRA). In the law are millions for "cronyism," such as for the National Quality Forum, a vain attempt to replace individuals' assessment of their quality of care along with their physicians with bureaucratic reporting and M.D. testing (Section 208).[263] Perhaps unknown to the legislature the entire board re-certifying industry has recently been exposed as nothing more than a moneymaking schema.[264] To the chagrin of many, the increases to physician payments are time limited and less than inflation. Unlike previous "fixes," this bill does add to the deficit, and intrusion on the patient-physician interaction becomes even more intense.*[265]

---

* Apparently Congress just cannot see itself out of Medicare being government-centered, with all the present difficulties within the legislative process, rather than a patient-centered program.

9

Misguided Good Intentions
the HITECH ACT and the PPACA

Section I: the HITECH Act

The Health Information Technology for Economic and Clinical Health Law, known as the HITECH Act, was part of the $787 billion stimulus package signed into law by President Obama on February 17, 2009. Approximately $20 billion of the $787 billion was devoted to this law.[266] An earlier 2005 RAND Corporation study sponsored by electronic health record companies and subsequently retracted, claimed that computerizing all medical records would supposedly save the healthcare industry $81 billion per year.[267] President Obama as part of the 2009 Stimulus Package touts the HITECH Act on February 17, 2009, but does not discuss possible shortcomings.[268] [269]

The law takes a carrot-and-stick approach. As an incentive to help recoup hardware and software costs, the law authorizes physicians treating Medicare patients to receive payments, up to approximately $48,000 in yearly increments provided they: 1) use certified electronic health records (CEHR), 2) adequately perform meaningful use (Tables 1-4), and 3) submit physician quality reporting data (PQRS).[270] The total payments are maximized if the physician starts the process in 2011, decreasing yearly becoming zero if adopted after 2015. Inadequate or absent PQRS reporting has penalties of decreased Medicare reimbursement. For practices with at least 30% Medicaid patients (20% for pediatricians), $65,000 in incentive payments would be received if the three above criteria were met by 2016.[271] Physicians may choose to participate in either reimbursement program, but not both. Hospitals may qualify for more than $2 million in reimbursements.[272] However, hospitals like physicians must also use programs certified by the Department of Health and Human Services (HHS) that meet various criteria determined by its Secretary and the Office of the National Coordinator for Health Information Technology.*[273] Some estimates are that for solo or small practices the cost for each physician for a certified program is about $40,000 and that for hospitals it is hundreds of millions of dollars.[274]

* Notice that physicians and hospitals are not certifying, or approving in any way, these certified electronic records or using the market to choose one to their liking; rather, it is the federal bureaucracy. This process is an example of regulatory capture that makes a few companies with political clout extremely profitable while excluding new and innovative competition.

Stage 1 Meaningful Use, which began in 2011, is defined for physicians as comprising 13 required core objectives, plus 5 objectives from a menu of 9, for a total of 18 objectives. Hospitals have 11 required core objectives, plus 5 objectives from a menu of 10, for a total of 16.[275]

Stage 2 Meaningful Use, which went into effect in 2014 requires a total of 20 objectives for physicians and 19 for hospitals. For physicians and hospitals to be eligible, they must also electronically report Clinical Quality Measures during each year of participation.[276][277]

The American Hospital Association, the American Medical Association, and the College of Healthcare Information Management Executives have all written to the Office of the National Coordinator for Health Information Technology to postpone the 2018 initiation of Stage 3 Meaningful Use until more is learned about the problems with Stage 1, chief among them cost and the inability to share information using different vendors' programs. The letters note that even after two years of trying, most hospitals and physicians have not been able to qualify for stage 1.[278] Is this a classic bait-and-switch: promise incentive payments, but make the necessary bureaucratic requirements so stringent that few will qualify for them? Here, the "stick" portion of the law operates via decreased Medicare payments if eligible professionals do not successfully participate in the program. Beginning in 2015 there will be a decrease in payment of 1%, increasing yearly to a maximum of 5%.[279] As almost all physicians and hospitals treat Medicare patients at a loss (see Chapter 7), this further decrease in payment would cause significant financial trouble for most providers. Therefore, this program is far from voluntary.

As an unintended consequence, it appears, paradoxically, that the HITECH Act has actually increased rather than decreased health care costs. As more physicians, because of the complexity of electronic medical records (EHR) compliance, leave private practice and become salaried by hospitals, the costs for services have dramatically increased.[280]

It is laudable to attempt to keep errors at an absolute minimum in an endeavor as complicated as medical care. It seems reasonable to expect that the uniform use of electronic medical records would help diminish errors in the less cognitive aspects of medicine. Electronic medical records perform well in informing clinicians about drug-drug interactions and any possible allergies. EHRs have proven to significantly improve vaccination rates because of the capacity to remind the caregiver at each visit of the need for such valuable preventative measures. Coupled with a computerized physician order entry system, medication errors have been dramatically reduced in some studies. Other studies, however, have demonstrated an increase in medication errors if the program interface is poorly designed, making it difficult for the clinician to enter the proper information.

One caveat to keep in mind is that most studies proving a benefit for these complex computer systems are conducted in large university medical centers that have had decades of experience with previous computerized systems, so that users have less need for extensive training.[281] Touted by the purveyors of these programs is the ability to expedite billing and payment by third parties. Whether yearly computer and program upkeep and licensing fees exceed the savings via expedited billing is an open question. A possible but as yet unproven benefit of having centralized aggregated data from EHRs would be having millions of patient data points regarding episodic outbreaks of infectious diseases such as influenza. Having this knowledge could allow public health officials to initiate mass vaccination at an earlier date.* Interoperability between programs from different vendors has remained a problem, as that has limited the goal of patients having a seamless record as they travel from center to center and from doctor to doctor.[282]

* The computer/programming industry is constantly improving its products and lowering costs. An open, free market without government picking favorites would have created choices that would have appealed to physicians and hospitals by substantially lowering costs and including even more features to improve patient care. Physicians would then have chosen systems that augmented their relationship with patients rather than impeding it. Competition would impel vendors to create programs that facilitate data entry in less time, instead of the excess time that is now required.

In favor of the HITECH Act, some have proposed that having "big data" on millions of patients will obviate the need for well-designed double blind, placebo- controlled trials in the advancement of medical science. I find this more of a wish than reality, however. This "big data" concept is counter to the scientific method (see chapter 1) of hypothesis testing with rigorous controls. Proponents are also underestimating the lack of validity of much of the data that are entered using these complex algorithms.

Limiting errors in physician judgment is a much more difficult task, which, notwithstanding some claims to the contrary, is not yet susceptible to improvement via EHRs. Errors may even be exacerbated by the currently available programs with cumbersome bureaucratic demands such as Meaningful use among others that take away from face time with the patient, including a careful history and physical exam, and from integrative thinking about the patient's unique situation.[283]

Of all misdiagnoses, the ten most common involve pulmonary embolism, drug reactions or overdoses, lung cancer, colorectal cancer, acute coronary syndromes, breast cancer, stroke, congestive heart failure, fractures, and abscess.[284] A 2008 study found a 17.2% major discrepancy identifying the cause of death in autopsies, and that missing a diagnosis not leading to death occurred in about 10% of all cases. The severe decline in autopsies has led to an overestimation of diagnostic performance and often misses nonlethal diagnostic errors.[285] The decline in autopsy rates is in part due to the false assumption that newer radiological techniques have obviated the need for autopsies. This is untrue, as CAT Scans and MRIs cannot provide microscopic diagnoses.* None of these important issues regarding physician errors are addressed by present federal requirements regarding electronic records.

> * This sharp drop in autopsy rates has, in my opinion, had a negative effect on physician training, causing a loss of emphasis on the pathologic mechanisms of disease.

Although penalties for physicians and hospitals violating electronic medical records privacy have been strengthened, that neglects the real threat, which is Internet piracy. Almost daily we read in the news about information in major computer systems having been hacked, and certainly hospitals and physicians are not immune. Unfortunately the HITECH Act made no provision for patient choice; participating physicians and hospitals must now have their medical records on the Internet. The alternative of having an individual's medical record on a personal storage device, perhaps password-protected, is not, at this time, an option.

There are many aspects of the present certified electronic medical records system that have been found problematic.[286] A recent study in *Medical Economics* of almost a thousand physicians found that:

1) *67% of respondents dissatisfied with system functionality*

2) *surprisingly almost 45% physicians have spent more than $100,000 for their EHR and 77% of large practices almost $200,000*

3) *there was an unexpected need to increase staff and loss in productivity*

4) *in practices with more than 10 physicians, 79% reported not worth the effort*

5) *45% of all respondents thought patient care is worse, 23% of internists' responded that patient care is significantly worse*

6) *69% reported that coordination with hospitals was not improved*

7) *65% claim that their EHRs are causing financial loss.*[287]

Physician difficulties with electronic medical records have been known for years, as well described by Drs. Hartzband and Groopman[288] —but it appears that the government and vendors did not take notice. They included:

- copying and pasting large quantities of text from previous sources, thereby inhibiting creative thought and creating an overly large and confusing volume of text;

- documentation for billing purposes, rather than for facilitating clear clinical thinking;

- perpetuating erroneous information, such as incorrect medications that can lead to serious patient complications;

- preoccupation with creating an electronic record at the expense of devoting attention and time to the patient;

- needing to fill in boxes for data entry, thereby inhibiting clear and incisive commentary; and

- overreliance on guidelines that prevent the necessary customization of care for each individual patient.

The authors noted that they were not against electronic medical records, but concluded that they should be created to augment rather than impede medical care, which is now the case.

An issue that seems to have received limited attention, which bodes poorly for the future skills of our physician workforce, is the concern that residency program directors have expressed (personal communications) with respect to the shift in the amount of time that residents are spending with patients versus with electronic medical records. A recent study found that residents spend about 12% of their time talking to and examining patients, versus more than 40% behind a computer.[289] Yet it is via hands-on patient contact that a young physician hones her or his skills.˙

> ˙ I, along with my senior colleagues and the program directors of Internal Medicine, are extremely concerned as we watch our trainees lose their history-taking and physical exam skills as their time with patients is being sacrificed to meet the needs of present-day EHRs. Because of the time needed by the teaching-attending to complete the medical record, there is significantly less time for trainee-attending interaction. This means greater reliance on laboratory and radiological tests, exposing patients to greater risks while driving up costs. Thus the rush to force the profession to use government-sanctioned EHRs or else experience payment reductions has the paradoxical potential of greatly increasing costs rather than fulfilling the original intent, which was to *limit* costs. There is no doubt that physicians and hospitals want to deliver safe, cost-efficient care to all patients and would surely use high-quality efficient electronic medical records as better versions become available. Larger hospitals have used some form of EHR for decades, and many were quite outstanding. It is disturbing that our lawmakers pass a sweeping bit of legislation, the HITECH Act that has had serious unintended consequences and yet undergoes no periodic review to rectify these many problems.

Drs. Patrick Ober and William Applegate recently published, *The electronic health record: Are we the tools of our tools?* They make several important points regarding our present use of "certified" electronic health records:

1) *the core of medicine is under attack; the computer and not the patient is now the main focus of the physician*

2) *patient-centered care has been replaced by computer-centered care, greatly impeding the patient-doctor healing relationship*

3) *physicians in training have been converted to "electronic processors"*

4) *we are in the process of eliminating individuality*

5) *time in the exam room must be entirely devoted to the patient*

6) *the nuances of each patient's individual story must be documented.*[290]

In summary the evidence is overwhelming: the HITECH Act has not accomplished any of its lofty goals, but has had a powerful negative effect on the practice of medicine in the U.S. Unfortunately our Congress with the passage of the Medicare Access and CHIP Reauthorization Act (MACRA) has made this situation even worse by increasing reporting requirements, thus taking even more time and energy away from concentrating on the patient's unique needs.

Section II: The Patient Protection and Affordable Care Act of 2010 (ACA)

America's health care problems are vast and deep and have taken decades to develop. The advent during World War II of employer-paid pre-tax health insurance put us on a course of third-party domination of health care. As these employee benefits continued to increase, the concept of insurance was distorted and morphed into prepaid care. Prepaid health care insulates the individual from any sense of cost, which actually encourages greater use of medical services regardless of need. Spending for health care, using taxpayers' dollars, increased exponentially with the passage of Medicare/Medicaid in 1965. As costs escalated, Medicare/Medicaid adopted a price-fixed system, thereby foregoing the discipline of the market. Nonetheless, costs continued to increase, causing Medicare and especially Medicaid to decrease reimbursement to hospitals, in many instances to below cost. Hospitals then charged private insurance increased amounts to recoup their federal program losses. Private insurance premiums paid mostly by employers or in the individual market, had to increase to cover these increased charges. As a result, premiums became too expensive for many, and the ranks of the uninsured grew to unacceptable levels. In addition, increased employer health care costs limited salary increases for employees.[291]

Physicians as a rule, unlike hospitals do not have the market strength to obtain increased amounts from private insurance, whose payment schedules mimic those of Medicare, thus decreasing their reimbursement. Within this price-fixing arrangement, payments for procedures have far outpaced non-procedural care. This policy has caused a massive disruption in the critical bond between physician and patient as time with each patient has dramatically diminished. With increased bureaucratic intrusion becoming more intense as a result of the HITECH Act, Affordable Care Act and MACRA, face time with patients has been further curtailed, along with an adequate history and physical exam and the necessary integrative thinking.[292] [293] As this has progressed, both patients and physicians feel increased insecurity, which in turn causes a far greater reliance on expensive testing, which again increases costs.

Taking care of patients is not the same as mass-producing cars, planes, computers, or anything else. Protocols are useful, but the care of every patient must be tailored to her or his specific needs. Unlike law, banking, or accounting, which likewise demand a host of cognitive skills, medicine also requires dedication, compassion, and caring—or, in the words of Sir William Osler, "equanimity, not disengagement." And compassion cannot be legislated; it must be respected and nurtured as a core value of medicine. The patient-doctor relationship is a human-to-human experience at a very deep level, and must not be destroyed by overwhelming bureaucratic burdens.

Paradoxically, as our government tries to control runaway costs by demanding medicine by rote, the essence of the physician-patient relationship suffers, and costs continue to escalate. Caring for patients with knowledge and compassion is not a modern relativistic idea, but rather is rooted in absolute values of service, dedication, honesty, and caring.[294] Any successful health care plan must nurture and enhance these values, not hinder them with ever-increasing levels of bureaucratic interference. Trying to control costs under the Affordable Care Act, many insurance companies unfortunately have restricted the choice of physicians, thus causing the dissolution of the bond between many patients and their doctor.[295] As the chronically ill represent approximately 10% of the population but consume approximately 80% of medical resources, shouldn't these patients have a choice to either stay with their primary care physician or receive all care under the direction of a specialist who has received further training and has greater expertise? This too would lower costs. But to be able to make this choice, patients would have to have greater control of their own health care dollars.

In this country, we would want a health care arrangement that does not create a multi-tiered system of the sort that is so prevalent in most, if not all, Western industrial countries. In these countries, government programs are always fighting cost restraints, resulting in long wait times and impersonal care. Those who can afford private insurance and out-of-pocket costs do so, as they pursue better, more attentive medical care. Coverage is not the same as care, as exemplified by the Medicaid program, with its well-documented shortcomings. A thoughtful change in our health care system would lessen the bureaucratic burden that is now costing us billions of dollars.[296]

Into this historic maze of sacrificing the patient-doctor relationship, escalating costs, more numbers of uninsured Americans, increasing federal and state budget concerns, and a number of those refused insurance because of pre-existing conditions, enter the PPACA, again built on an even more extensive government platform. The law as written is approximately 2,700 pages, which have engendered about 13,000 pages of regulations.[297] There were two often stated major goals for creating this law: to decrease the escalating costs of health care and to insure all Americans.[298]

Here we will review general features of the Law[299]

1) A Health Insurance Marketplace (electronic, phone or paper) comparing prices-benefits from participating insurance companies.

> *Problems –*
>
> a) *Difficulty for many people because of the construct of the healthcare.gov web site, determining eligibility before describing options.[300]*
>
> b) *The financial losses many states incurred as their ACA exchange failed to work in a timely and appropriate manner caused the U.S. Senate to hold a hearing subtitled, A Closer Look at the Hundreds of Millions of Taxpayer Dollars Wasted.[301]*
>
> c) *The question of whether the ACA law as written permits the IRS to make available subsidies on the Federal versus State exchanges has been reviewed.[302] The Supreme Court, after conflicting findings in lower courts, reviewed this question in March 2015 with a finding expected in June, if found that the IRS had no authority to provide*

subsidies on the Federal exchange, these funds will probably have to be reclaimed by the IRS. Congress is working to address this possibility should it occur.[303] Note added in proof, the Supreme Court found that subsidies WERE legal on state AND federal exchanges.

d) *Because of delayed income verification upon rollout, underreporting or change in income during the year will mean owing the IRS monies for million/s of those receiving subsidies.[304]*

e) *Insurance brokers who are small business people and who are licensed and knowledgeable regarding appropriateness of insurance needs for individuals and families, will be put out-of-business by the exchanges of the Affordable Care Act.[305]*

2) Preventive services will have no out-of-pocket costs, including many for women.

Problems –

a) *Thought of by many as cost saving, preventative measures practiced on an entire population rather than selectively applied to those at greater risk is both wasteful of resources and crowds out time for caring for the truly ill.[306] Massive screening also increases the likelihood of false positives.[307]*

b) *Perpetuates our society's confusion between health insurance and pre-paid health care. Even some of the most learned among us have made this mistake. Insurance is meant to pay for big-ticket items – an example is homeowners insurance, which pays for houses on fire not for routine maintenance such as painting the exterior. Having pre-paid health care is one of the major reasons our health costs are unsustainable, in part by obfuscating the real price of items. It is also unfair for those who do not or cannot benefit from a medical service to be forced to pay for it by a third party. Rather our society should make sure that all have the financial means to pay for needed screening and maintenance via health savings accounts. Certainly all women wishing birth control should have the means to obtain whatever they and their doctor decide. However, it should not become a Supreme Court issue as in the Hobby Lobby case if all women were spending their own money from their health account. It certainly is nobody else's business to know or decide what an individual woman wishes regarding birth control.*[308]

c) *Having no out-of-pocket costs does not mean these services are free. They just increase the cost of premiums.*

3) So called essential health benefits to be included in most health insurance plans; there are many.[309] They are:

1) *Ambulatory services*

2) *Emergency services*

3) *Prescription services*

4) *Hospitalization*

5) *Rehabilitative services and devices*

6) *Maternity and new born care*

7) *Laboratory services*

8) *Mental health/substance abuse*

9) *Preventive/wellness services and chronic disease management*

10) *Pediatric services, including oral and vision care*

Problem –

Rather surprising that the ACA would contain multiple mandates that have been known to drive up the costs of coverage at the state level for years. These mandates drive up the price of health maintenance coverage, by including options that many people will never use –e.g., maternity care for men.[310]

4) Adult children up to age 26 can be included on your health insurance plan.

>   ***Problem –***
>
>   *Sounds good, but of course you are paying for it with higher premiums; nothing is for free.[311]*

5) Free to choose your doctor

>   ***Problem –***
>
>   *The statement, "You Choose your doctor", had to be qualified for many patients; because of the complexities of the ACA, free choice of physician in many cases is no longer true. As third party payers have dealt with pricing issues within the law, they have responded by limiting the panel of physicians and hospitals available under their plans. The promise, "you can keep your doctor if you wish" has not materialized.[312]*

6) Emergency access guaranteed

>   ***Problem –***
>
>   *This is disingenuous, as any emergency room access has been guaranteed regardless of the ability to pay by law since 1986 by passage of the Emergency Medical Treatment and Active Labor Act.[313]*

7) The law makes it easier to understand health care coverage

>   ***Problem –***
>
>   *The ACA has been a disaster for those small business people who were in the health insurance brokerage business. Yes a summary may be of benefit, but it is no substitute for an expert guiding an individual or family as to the best coverage at the best price to meet their needs. Navigators charged with helping people navigate the ACA exchanges are not trained to the extent of insurance brokers and are not face-to-face as trusted professionals.[314]*

8) Ability to appeal if coverage is denied.

> *After reviewing your denials by your health insurance company it can be reviewed independently.*

Problem – None

So far, what is the evidence that the ACA has achieved its two major goals of 1) decreasing the nation's spending on health care and 2) insuring all Americans?

1) From CMS.gov: "Health spending is projected to grow at an average rate of 5.8 percent from 2012-2022, 1.0 percentage point faster than expected average annual growth in the Gross Domestic Product (GDP)."[315] It appears that the ACA has not been effective in decreasing national health care costs.[316]

2) The number of uninsured in America by 2024 is estimated to be about 40 million, roughly 10% more than at this time.[317] This may be a high estimate, but all such estimates are in the multiple millions. Thus this law will not meet the second goal of universal coverage.

Summary of the HITECH and Patient Protection and Affordable Care Acts

Physicians practice evidence-based medicine within the limits of individual variability. But we as taxpayers do not ask our political leaders to practice evidence-based national policy whenever possible. These two laws, the HITECH Act and the ACA, involve the expenditure of massive amounts of dollars and human energy. Yet like many other federal programs, they were enacted in full rather than initially field-tested in smaller increments, so that the inevitable unintended consequences could be recognized and the feasibility of achieving the initial goals evaluated. Hopefully in the future our political leaders will see the folly of their ways and carefully evaluate their legislative initiatives resulting in laws not based on beliefs, but rather on reality.

I am in total agreement with those who wish to make healthcare available and affordable to ALL Americans. The problem is that a concept initiated in the 1880's of a benefit rather than a payment has fostered a top down, immensely bureaucratic, impersonal, excessively expensive system. Rather, put the patient at the center of the system by ensuring all have the financial resources to direct their own care and to choose the medical services that meet their specific needs.

Table 1

Meaningful Use: Eligible Professionals (Stage 1)
Core Objectives (choose 13)

(https://www.cms.gov/Regulations-and-Guidance/Legislation/EHRIncentivePrograms/downloads/MU_Stage1_ReqOverview.pdf):

1) *Computerized provider order entry (CPOE)*
2) *E-Prescribing (eRx)*
3) *Report ambulatory clinical quality measures to CMS/States*
4) *Implement one clinical decision support rule*
5) *Provide patients with an electronic copy of their health information, upon request*
6) *Provide clinical summaries for patients for each office visit*
7) *Drug-drug and drug-allergy interaction checks*
8) *Record demographics*
9) *Maintain an up-to-date problem list of current and active diagnoses*
10) *Maintain active medication list*
11) *Maintain active medication allergy list*
12) *Record and chart changes in vital signs*
13) *Record smoking status for patients 13 years or older*
14) *Capability to exchange key clinical information among providers of care and patient-authorized entities electronically*
15) *Protect electronic health information*

Table 2 (Stage 1)

Eligible Professionals – 10 Menu Objectives (choose 3)

https://www.cms.gov/Regulations-and-Guidance/ Legislation/EHRIncentivePrograms/downloads/MU_ Stage1_ReqOverview.pdf

d) *Drug-formulary checks*

e) *Incorporate clinical lab test results as structured data*

f) *Generate lists of patients by specific conditions*

g) *Send reminders to patients per patient preference for preventive/follow up care*

h) *Provide patients with timely electronic access to their health information*

i) *Use certified EHR technology to identify patient-specific education resources and provide to patient, if appropriate*

j) *Medication reconciliation*

k) *Summary of care record for each transition of care/referrals*

l) *Capability to submit electronic data to immunization registries/systems**

m) *Capability to provide electronic syndromic surveillance data to public health agencies* * At least 1 public health objective must be selected.*

Table 3 (stage 1)

14 Hospital Core Objectives (choices)

https://www.cms.gov/Regulations-and-Guidance/ Legislation/EHRIncentivePrograms/downloads/MU_ Stage1_ReqOverview.pdf

1) *Computerized provider order entry (CPOE)*

2) *Drug-drug and drug-allergy interaction checks*

3) *Record demographics*

4) *Implement one clinical decision support rule*

5) *Maintain up-to-date problem list of current and active diagnosis*

6) *Maintain active medication list*

7) *Maintain active medication allergy list*

8) *Record and chart changes in vital signs*

9) *Record smoking status for patients 13 years or older*

10) *Report hospital clinical quality measures to CMS or States*

11) *Provide patients with an electronic copy of their health information, upon request*

12) *Provide patients with an electronic copy of their discharge instructions at time of discharge, upon request*

13) *Capability to exchange key clinical information among providers of care and patient-authorized entities electronically*

14) *Protect electronic health information*

Table 4 (stage 1)

Hospitals – 10 Menu Objectives (choices)

https://www.cms.gov/Regulations-and-Guidance/ Legislation/EHRIncentivePrograms/downloads/MU_ Stage1_ReqOverview.pdf

1) *Drug-formulary checks*

2) *Record advanced directives for patients 65 years or older*

3) *Incorporate clinical lab test results as structured data*

4) *Generate lists of patients by specific conditions*

5) *Use certified EHR technology to identify patient-*

specific education resources and provide to patient, if appropriate

6) *Medication reconciliation*

7) *Summary of care record for each transition of care/referrals*

8) *Capability to submit electronic data to immunization registries/systems**

9) *Capability to provide electronic submission of reportable lab results to public health agencies**

10) *Capability to provide electronic syndromic surveillance data to public health agencies**
* At least 1 public health objective must be selected.

10
THE NEXT STEP – FREEDOM IN HEALTHCARE

A frequently heard refrain from many "experts" is that in healthcare, markets unlike in other commodities do not work. This concept was given credence by a 1963 article written by the Nobel Prize winning economist Kenneth Arrow.[318] Professor Arrow's five points were:

1) *unpredictability – frequently our need for healthcare is unexpected and urgent*

2) *barriers to entry – one cannot just put up a sign and practice medicine; it takes years of education and licensing, thus diminishing supply*

3) *the importance of trust – patients must trust the competence of a physician, especially with procedures*

4) *asymmetrical information – because doctors usually know far more than their patients, their advice is frequently blindly followed and government or other 3rd parties are too removed to determine appropriateness*

5) *idiosyncrasies of payment – payment takes place after the service; patients have little information of cost and rarely pay for services directly.*[319]

* Professor Arrow also had no knowledge of the upcoming information age, with its attendant increase in patient knowledge, thereby significantly decreasing this asymmetry. The knowledge missing is price transparency and market forces fostered by a price-fixed centralized government system.

But, are these parameters really different than other market transactions that we undergo every day and does a distant bureaucracy make it better or worse? This was explored in an article published in 2012 in The Atlantic by Avik Roy,[320] which analyzed the five points:

1) *unpredictability – not unique to health care; many occasions occur suddenly, but are addressed by warranties on various products and with old-*

fashioned insurance

2) *barriers to entry of practitioners with licensing – licensing is common with lawyers, dentists and in many other activities such as animal grooming, hair dressers and barbers, etc. yet there is no claim to make these a government dominated function*

3) *trust – when purchasing any product such as cars, airplane tickets, etc we trust that the product is safe*

4) *asymmetry of knowledge – is not unique to healthcare; most of us cannot take apart then rebuild an automobile, a computer, a television, but we shop for value using price transparency*

5) *idiosyncrasies of payment – indeed this is the problem; prepaid healthcare has become more entrenched since Arrow's paper in 1963. Instead of suggesting more government control, the solution should have advocated more patient-centered control.*[321]

Others besides Kenneth Arrow contend that a patient cannot always shop for healthcare, for instance when having a heart attack or other acute serious event. However, in 2013, 32.1% of total healthcare spending was for hospital care, and certainly not all was on an emergency basis.[322] Thus less than the 32.1% of healthcare spending is for acute problems. If the industry were structured like all others, price transparency and patient choice would be in effect for the remaining issues, thus controlling costs.

Proving that markets do work in healthcare in this country is the spectacular growth of health savings accounts along with high deductible insurance.[323] With these accounts patients use tax-free dollars for their routine healthcare needs as they shop for the best value, using their insurance only for big-ticket items.

Instead for a vast majority of Americans with our present price-fixed, pre-paid, government dominated, third party healthcare system we have:

1) *perverse incentives that encourage excess treatments that plague our system, especially Medicare[324]*

2) *excessive costs*

3) *inferior service*

4) *a mistake-prone system*

5) *no incentives to control costs and increase efficiency*

6) *neglecting other critical societal needs*

7) *extreme complexity*

8) *many left with no or inadequate insurance.[325]*

Change to mostly patient directed care will be difficult for many to accept. The Congress has been at the center of health care for over 50 years giving their members relevance, various talking points, the center of a great deal of lobbying activity and access to considerable campaign financing. Other major players such as health insurance companies, the pharmaceutical industry and "certified" electronic health record providers have been extremely successful lobbying for great economic advantage in this government centered, price-controlled system. Established physician organizations have become convinced that our government is the source of physician income and thus tout the government line. The academic "experts" who testify before Congress have built their careers becoming well versed in the intricacies of our convoluted government controlled system. All these entities will find it difficult to change to a patient-centered health care system regardless of its logic, better care and less cost.

It is in the interest of our society for each member to be as healthy and productive as possible. This can happen only if every citizen has the possibility of having excellent up-to-the-minute health care—and the cornerstone of such care is an active therapeutic relationship with a skillful, knowledgeable, compassionate physician. Our task is to create a system whereby every American has an equal opportunity to have this type of healing relationship, thereby maximizing health while at the same time conserving resources.

We could have a healthcare system that offers equal and better care for all, as opposed to the present multi-tiered entity, with all of its attendant problems.

In the United States we now have a five-tiered health care system: the uninsured, Medicaid, Medicare, private insurance and those on the exchanges with narrow networks and increasingly unaffordable deductions. The uninsured and Medicaid patients, as discussed in chapter 8, have the greatest problems in terms of access and poor health outcomes. Some Medicare patients are also experiencing access problems that will substantially worsen if the decreases in reimbursement included in the Affordable Care Act (ACA) actually take place.[326] Patients with private insurance have the best access, although with the advent of the ACA, insurance companies are limiting hospital and physician choice along with increasing deductibles in order to control costs.[327] The cost of health care and the complexity of the present system must also be addressed.

Solution: A voluntary program for all Americans—uninsured, Medicaid, Medicare, and privately insured—to enable anyone who wishes to forgo third-party-dominated healthcare. Citizens could choose between their present plans or a health savings account (HSA), funded by a universally available refundable tax credit increasing with age from the federal government and high-deductible health insurance plan (HDHP).[328]

Individuals could add to their HSA with after tax dollars if they so wish; the account would grow tax free as would be withdrawal for health care issues. A plan of this nature would not require full repeal of the Affordable Care Act, but repeal of the mandates and the Independent Payment Advisory Board would be most helpful.

HSAs, which are permitted under the Affordable Care Act, should be expanded so that payments for HDHPs and direct care contracts would be paid out of those accounts.[329] Direct care contracts are between a patient and her or his chosen physician, usually paid on a monthly basis varying in cost depending on several variables from about $30 to $100/month.[330]

Frequently this includes standard yearly lab work, approximately twenty-five visits a year, and discounted testing.[331] Several states have passed laws making direct care contracts more available by stating that they are NOT insurance, thus avoiding the myriad of state regulations.[332] HDHPs should be available on a national level, avoiding the many state mandates that drive up the cost of health insurance; that would also ensure complete portability.[333] After death, any remaining funds in the HSA should be able to be passed on into another living person's HSA, as per the patient's instructions. To resolve disputes in the unusual instance when a family desires a premature death in order to acquire the accumulated funds, there would be recourse to the courts. Invariably the courts find in favor of the continuance of care.[334]

How can those without or with meager income, about 17 percent of our population, fund their HSAs? This would take place via a refundable tax credit directly deposited into their HSA that would also include a HDHP in a manner similar to Switzerland,[335] Singapore,[336] and previously in the state of Indiana.[337] The federal government share of Medicaid could be provided directly into each person's account or to the states as block grants. The states, if needed could augment these funds, depositing additional money in each person's HSA assuring adequate funds for their HDHPs and direct care contracts. Experience with this method has demonstrated increased patient satisfaction, decreasing emergency room visits, and considerable lessening of costs.[338] In 2013 about 27 million working families and individuals received the earned income tax credit; those monies, or a fraction thereof, combined with the healthcare tax credit could be transferred directly into their HSAs.[339] Employers could augment those funds by contributing directly into their employees' HSAs to assure adequately funded accounts to pay for HDHPs and direct care contracts. To accomplish this, HSAs would need modification by Congress. As this would cost employers much less than current health insurance, one of the major reasons for employee salary stagnation would be ameliorated, while federal expenditures for this group could be minimized.[340] This would also eliminate the need for the problematic ACA exchanges and the Act's expensive taxpayer-funded subsidies.

All of these transactions would be accomplished using pre-tax dollars and would eliminate any concern for problems regarding pre-existing conditions, in accordance with the HIPPA law of 1996.[341] About 50 percent of the population pays federal income taxes; they would receive the healthcare tax credit to fund their HSA, with an arrangement with the employer for the augmentation of their account.[342] Payroll withholding for Medicare could gradually over decades transfer to an individual's separate health account. This account would not be accessible till after age 65. Thus after an initial phase-in period for most Americans, there would be ample funds to be used for healthcare after retirement. The HSA for each family member would be in each individual's name, so children would be accumulating funds from birth. Following proposed IRS guidelines monies in the account must be carefully invested in a conservative mix of stocks and bonds. The bonds would protect the account from large market declines and also help fund the national debt, eventually eliminating foreign participation. People could also stay with their HDHP for a lifetime, which premiums would actuarially assure their care when older. This capital accumulation eventually providing healthcare for most after retirement would relieve the federal government of its present Medicare obligations.

It would then be in the financial interest of insurance companies to foster healthy life-styles, thereby increasing their profits. But a fraction of the population will succumb to expensive disease long before retirement.[343] Under this plan, the HDHPs would charge enough to fund additional reinsurance accounts. These accounts would also actuarially augment funds in the unfortunate individual's HSA in order to cover increased expenses. In this way, the individual remains in charge of her or his care and sensitive to price. In effect, it is a reinsurance fund to ensure that individuals have the capability for funding their care along with their augmented HDHP. The reinsurance charges must be adequate to cover catastrophic expenses, such as for patients needing heart, liver, and kidney transplants. Notice that once the government directly or indirectly funds HSA accounts, the individual citizen is then in charge of her or his health care, rather than bureaucrats in Washington. It is possible that catastrophic costs for an elderly person could exhaust funds that have been saved over the years; either the special HDHP funds could meet that need or, in an extreme circumstance, the federal government could maintain a small account for this purpose, financed by general tax revenues.

This plan providing access for all Americans would decrease our health care costs. It is axiomatic that all of us are much more careful spending our own money than we are with everybody else's. Complete cost transparency would be required with physicians and hospitals paid market prices for their services—a dramatic change from our present price-fixed system. Under this universal system there would be no uncompensated care. Thus, hospitals would no longer need to be not-for-profit and would be taxed like any other entity. They would have to compete on service and price. New entrepreneurial facilities offering superior services would most likely be created along with the disappearance of outdated certificate of need laws.[344] [345] Hospitals would soon learn to compete like all other enterprises and would add substantially to local, state, and federal tax coffers.

My plan has many similarities to that recently published by the Pacific Research Institute.[346] A major difference is that with my plan I would give employees a choice. Employees could change their insurance and opt for a tax credited HSA-HDHP account. As this would be a new option, I expect that initially many would be skeptical, but over time almost everyone would want the advantages of controlling their own healthcare dollars.

There is a need to strengthen and nurture the therapeutic patient-doctor relationship.

Historically, physicians have cared for patients applying skills and knowledge with compassion, understanding, and empathy. There is no doubt that a strong patient-doctor therapeutic relationship improves care and leads to better results.[347] This plan would ameliorate the increasing dominance of third-party prepaid medicine as described in chapter 9, which is compromising this relationship.

Patients in charge of their own funds under this HSA-HDHP system would be able to seek out a compatible physician to meet their needs. Patients and their physicians together would control the amount of time needed for each visit, with payment adjusted accordingly; this does not happen in the present third-party prepaid health care system.[348] Physicians and hospitals would be free to choose a patient record system that enhances patient and physician needs rather than fulfilling artificial requirements (presently called meaningful use and now MACRA).[349] Patients spending their own money would pay more attention to maximizing their health, thus decreasing their spending. This is the pathway to improving population health, one patient at a time, rather than the present bureaucratic attempts to accomplish this goal.[350] Presently there is electronic reporting of patient information in the event of adverse outcomes involving various therapeutic agents; that practice should be retained.[351] When there is participation in National Institute of Health clinical or other trials, electronic reporting must take place as directed by the research protocol.

We need to determine if there really is a Primary Care shortage.

Presently we do not know whether a primary care shortage exists. This is because there has not been patient market choice to meet the needs of those with chronic disease, who make up about 10% of the population. We do know that there are now more physicians per 100,000 population in the United States than at any other time in our history.[352] Certainly physicians trained as Internal Medicine and Neurological subspecialists could, if patients with chronic disease so desired, meet their primary care needs, thus decreasing demand on other physicians. The choice of primary care by graduating medical students under this HSA-HDHP system, with a greater emphasis on patient relationships and enhanced incomes, would be more appealing than at the present time. But only in a true market system will we know the answer to the primary care question. And only in a market system will we be able to determine if our nation has a greater or lesser need for primary care vis-à-vis specialty-trained physicians.

With individual choice we could have a brighter health care future.

If, as I suspect, a majority of Americans choose the self-directed HSA-HDHP option, health care in this country will significantly improve, especially for the poor, and there will be a large decrease in the national cost of health care.[353] Our decades-long divisive health care debate would finally be over. We could then focus more on the most important task facing any society: creating an educational system that ensures that every child, to the maximum of their ability, has the skills to successfully participate in the now worldwide industrial economy. This would require a much more intense educational system than exists at the present time and would require more funding. With health care consuming approximately 18% of gross domestic product this funding would prove elusive. An HSA-HDHP system would allow us to spend less on health care and more on our future.

Further Reading

1) Morris Fishbein, M.D., *A History of The American Medical Association 1847 To 1947*, Philadelphia & London: W.B. Saunders Company, 1947

2) Albert Lyons S., M.D., Joseph R. Petrucelli, II, M.D. *MEDICINE: An Illustrated History*, New York: Harry N. Abrams, INC., 1978

3) Frank D. Campion, *The AMA And U.S. Health Policy: Since 1940*, Chicago: Chicago Review Press, 1984

4) Ann G. Carmichael, Richard M. Ratzan editors, *Medicine: A Treasury Of Art And Literature*, New York: Hugh Lauter Levin Associates, Inc. & Macmillan Publishing Company, 1991

5) John Duffy, *From Humors to Medical Science: A History of American Medicine, 2nd Edition*, Urbana and Chicago: University of Illinois Press, 1993

6) Irvine Loudon, Editor. *Western Medicine: An Illustrated History*, Oxford & New York: Oxford University Press, 1997

7) John P. Seward M.D., *Caring for the Country: A History and Celebration of the First 150 Years of the American Medical Association*, Chicago: American Medical Association, 1997

8) Regina Herzlinger, *Who Killed Health Care?: America's $2 Trillion Medical Problem – And The Consumer- Driven Cure*, New York, London, etc. : McGraw-Hill, 2007

9) John F. Hunt. M.D., *Assume The Physician: Modern Medicine's "Catch-22"*, Kimberly Johnson – www.readjohnhunt.com, 2012

10) John C. Goodman, *Priceless: Curing The Healthcare Crisis*, Oakland California: The Independent Institute, 2012

11) David Goldhill, *Catastrophic Care: Why Everything We Think We Know About Health Care Is Wrong*, New York: Vintage Books, 2013

12) Christopher J. Conover, *American Health Economy: Illustrated*, Washington, D.C. : AEI Press, 2012

13) Avik Roy, *How Medicaid Fails The Poor*, New York: Encounter Books, 2013

14) James C. Mohr, *Licensed to Practice: The Supreme Court Defines The American Medical Profession*, Baltimore: The Johns Hopkins University Press, 2013

NOTES

1.William Osler, The Principles and Practice of Medicine: Designed for the Use of Practitioners and Students of Medicine (New York: D. Appleton, 1892).

2.Rockefeller University, "History of the Rockefeller University," http://www.rockefeller.edu/about/history. (Accessed 1/10/2013).

3 David McCullough, The Greater Journey: Americans in Paris (New York: Simon & Schuster, 2011), p. 135

4 Encyclopedia Britannica, "National Health Service (NHS)," (October 7, 2013). http://www.britannica.com/EBchecked/topic/404901/National-Health-Service-NHS. (Accessed 1/12/2013).

5 Nobelprize.org, "Award Ceremony Speech," 1977, available on line, http://www.nobelprize.org/nobel_prizes/medicine/laureates/1977/presentation-speech.html (Accessed 9/27/2013)

6 Abby Cessna, "Geocentric Model" (2009), http://www.universetoday.com/32607/geocentric-model/ (Accessed 9/18/2013).

7 Top Universities: Worldwide University Rankings, Guides & Events: "University of Padua," http://www.topuniversities.com/universities/university-padua/undergrad (Accessed 10/7/2013).

8 Edward Rosen, Three Copernican Treatises, 3rd ed. (New York, Octagon Books, 1971), p. 353.

9 W. Bogdanowicz, M. Allen, W. Branicki, et al., "Genetic Identification of Putative Remains of the Famous Astronomer Nicolaus Copernicus," PNAS 106, 30 (2009): 12,279 12,282.

10 N. P. Leveillee, "Copernicus, Galileo, and the Church: Science in a Religious World" (2011), http://www.studentpulse.com/articles/533/copernicus-galileo-and-the-church-science-in-a-religious-world (Accessed 10/2/2013).

11 Sheila Rabin, "Nicolaus Copernicus" (2010), Stanford Encyclopedia of Philosophy, http://plato.stanford.edu/entries/copernicus/ (Accessed 9/25/2013).

12 Understanding Evolution: "Comparative Anatomy: Andreas Vesalius" (2013), University of California Museum of Paleontology, http://evolution.berkeley.edu/evolibrary/article/history_02 (Accessed 10/1/2013).

13 William Bristow, "Enlightenment" (August 20, 2010), Stanford Encyclopedia of Philosophy, http://plato.stanford.edu/entries/enlightenment/ (Accessed 3/15/13).

14 Paul Brians, "The Enlightenment" (May 18, 2000), http://public.wsu.edu/~brians/hum_303/enlightenment.html (Accessed 1/21/2013).

15 Merriam-Webster.com, s.v. "Deism," http://www.merriam-webster.com/dictionary/deism (Accessed 11/5/2014).

16 Paul Brians, "Romanticism" (October 1, 2004), http://public.wsu.edu/~brians/hum_303/romanticism.html (Accessed 1/22/2013).

17 "Medical School at Salerno," http://health.yodelout.com/medical-school-at-salerno/ (Accessed 3/15/2013).

18 David K. Osborn, "The Four Humors" (2010), http://www.greekmedicine.net/b_p/Four_Humors.html (Accessed 3/15/2013).

19 "The Death of George Washington," Digital Encyclopedia of George Washington (Accessed 11/5/2014).

20 "The History of Medicine 1800–1850" (2003), International Wellness Directory, http://www.mnwelldir.org/docs/history/history03.htm (Accessed 1/22/2013).

21 Albert S. Lyons,and R. Joseph Petrucelli, Medicine: An Illustrated History (New York: Abrams, 1978), p. 496.

22 Ibid., p. 493.

23 Elizabeth A. Fenn, Small Pox and the American Revolution, www.dlt.ncssm.edu/lmtm/docs/smallpox/Script.doc (Accessed 1/23/2013).

24 BBC: History,"Edward Jenner (1749–1823)" (2013), http://www.bbc.co.uk/history/his-

toric_figures/jenner_edward.shtml (Accessed 1/24/2013).

25 Harold Cook, "From the Scientific Revolution to the Germ Theory," in *Western Medicine: An Illustrated History*, ed. Irvine Loudon (New York: Oxford University Press, 1997), p. 89.

26 Edward Jenner, "An Inquiry into the Causes and Effects . . . of the Cow-Pox," in *Medicine: A Treasury of Art and Literature*, ed. Ann G. Carmichael and Richard M. Ratzan (New York: Hugh Lauter Associates, distributed by Macmillan, 1991), pp. 131–33.

27 "Medical Advances Timeline" (2007), http://www.infoplease.com/ipa/A0932661.html (Accessed 1/25/2013).

28 Rene T. H. Laennec, "The Invention of the Stethoscope," in Carmichael and Ratzan, *Medicine*, pp. 134–35.

29 Wittern-Sterzel, R (2003). "Politics is nothing else than large scale medicine"—Rudolf Virchow and his role in the development of social medicine". Verhandlungen der Deutschen Gesellschaft *fur Pathologie* **87**: 150–157. PMID 16888907 (Accessed 10/30/2013).

30 The Wood-Library-Museum, "The History of Anesthesia", available at, http://www.wood-librarymuseum.org/history-of-anesthesia/ (Accessed 1/21/2016).

31 "Long, Crawford" (2013), http://georgiainfo.galileo.usg.edu/longbio.htm (Accessed 1/26/2013).

32 UCLA Dept. of Epidemiology: School of Public Health, "Anesthesia and Queen Victoria," http://www.ph.ucla.edu/epi/snow/victoria.html (Accessed 10/22/2013).

33 Lyons and Petrucelli. *Medicine*, pp. 527–31.

34 Centers for Disease Control and Prevention, "Cholera: Vibrio cholerae Infection," *http://www.cdc.gov/cholera/index.html* (Accessed 1/27/2013).

35 John Snow Archive and Research Companion, "About John Snow," http://johnsnow.matrix.msu.edu/aboutjohn.php (Accessed 1/28/2013).

36 BBC: History, "John Snow (1813–1858)," http://www.bbc.co.uk/history/historic_figures/snow_john.shtml (Accessed 10/23/2013).

37 NCBI, Dunn P.M. "Oliver Wendell Holmes (1809-1894) and his Essay On Pueral Fever," http://www.ncbi.nlm.nih.gov/pmc/articles/PMC2675443/ (Accessed 3/21/2015).

38 Ignaz Semmelweis, "The Etiology, Concept, and Prophylaxis of Childbed Fever: Autobiographical Introduction," in Carmichael and Ratzan, *Medicine*, pp. 136–47.

39 Lyons and Petrucelli. *Medicine*, pp. 556–57.

40 Louis Pasteur. (2015). The Biography.com website. Retrieved 12:35, Mar 21, 2015, from http://www.biography.com/people/louis-pasteur-9434402.

41 Association of the British Pharmaceutical Industry, *Resources for Schools:* Infectious diseases—timeline; "Joseph Lister and Antiseptic Surgery," http://www.abpischools.org.uk/page/modules/infectiousdiseases_timeline/timeline5.cfm?coSiteNavigation_allTopic=1 (Accessed 3/16/2013).

42 University of Maryland. "Koch's Postulates to Identify the Causative Agent of an Infectious Disease," http://www.life.umd.edu/classroom/bsci424/BSCI223WebSiteFiles/KochsPostulates.htm (Accessed 10/29/2013).

43 Science Museum: Brought to Life; Exploring the History of Medicine, "Robert Koch (1843–1910)," http://www.sciencemuseum.org.uk/broughttolife/people/robertkoch.aspx (Accessed 2/4/2013).

44 University of Maryland, "Koch's Postulates," http://www.life.umd.edu/classroom/bsci424/BSCI223WebSiteFiles/KochsPostulates.htm (Accessed 10/30/2013).

45 History Learning Site, "Alexander Fleming and Penicillin," http://www.historylearningsite.co.uk/alexander_fleming_and_penicillin.htm (Accessed 10/22/2013).

46 NPR, "Antibiiotics Can't Keep Up With 'Nightmare' Superbugs" (October 22, 2013), http://www.npr.org/2013/10/22/239247134/antibiotics-cant-keep-up-with-nightmare-superbugs (Accessed 10/23/2013).

47 Lyons and Petrucelli. *Medicine*, p. 559.

48 "Ronald Ross: Biographical," http://www.nobelprize.org/nobel_prizes/medicine/laureates/1902/ross-bio.html (Accessed 2/6/2013).

49 Medical News Today, "Global Malaria Battle Loses Steam" (December 18, 2012), http://www.medicalnewstoday.com/articles/254165.php (Accessed 10/24/2013).

50 "Wilhelm Conrad Röntgen: Biographical" , http://www.nobelprize.org/nobel_prizes/physics/laureates/1901/rontgen-bio.html (Accessed 2/4/2013).

51 "Riva-Rocci Sphygmomanometer," http://woodlibrarymuseum.org/museum/item/14/riva-rocci-sphygmomanometer (Accessed 2/5/2013).

52 Irvine Loudon, *Western Medicine: An Illustrated History* (New York: Oxford University Press, 1997), p. 321.

53 Cherry Kendra, "The Id, Ego and Superego: The Structural Model of Personality," http://psychology.about.com/od/theoriesofpersonality/a/personalityelem.htm (Accessed 10/29/2013).

54 Cherry Kendra, "Sigmund Freud: Life, Work and Theories," http://psychology.about.com/od/sigmundfreud/p/sigmund_freud.htm (Accessed 10/20/2013).

55 Amy Sue Bix, introduction to Elizabeth Blackwell, *Pioneer Work in Opening the Medical Profession to Women* , (orig. 1895; Amherst, NY: Humanity Books, 2005), p. 24.

56 National Library of Medicine, "Dr. Elizabeth Blackwell," http://www.nlm.nih.gov/changingthefaceofmedicine/physicians/biography_35.html (Accessed 10/27/2013).

57 David McCullough, *The Greater Journey: An American In Paris* (New York, Simon & Schuster, 2011), pp. 191–94.

58 *Encyclopedia Britannica*, "New York Infirmary for Women and Children," http://www.britannica.com/EBchecked/topic/412455/New-York-Infirmary-for-Women-and-Children (Accessed 10/25/2013).

59 National Women's History Museum, "Elizabeth Blackwell (1821-1910)," http://www.nwhm.org/education-resources/biography/biographies/elizabeth-blackwell/ (Accessed 10/28/2013).

60 "Medical College of Pennsylvania," http://www.infoplease.com/encyclopedia/society/medical-college-pennsylvania.html (Accessed 10/25/2013).

61 National Library of Medicine, "Dr. Rebecca Lee Crumpler," http://www.nlm.nih.gov/changingthefaceofmedicine/physicians/biography_73.html (Accessed 10/28/2013).

62 Susan La Flesche Picotte. [Internet]. 2015. The Biography.com website. Available from: http://www.biography.com/people/susan-la-flesche-picotte-9440355 [Accessed 21 Mar 2015].

63 Johns Hopkins Magazine, "A Timeline of Women at Hopkins," Available from: http://pages.jh.edu/~jhumag/1107web/women2.html (Accessed 3/21/2015).

64 Changing The Face of Medicine, "Dr. Eliza Ann Grier" Available from: https://www.nlm.nih.gov/changingthefaceofmedicine/physicians/biography_132.html (Accessed 3/21/2015).

65 Martha R. Clevenger, Bernard Becker Medical Library Digital Collection, "From Lay Practitioner to Doctor of Medicine: Women Physicians in St. Louis, 1860 – 1920", available at, http://beckerexhibits.wustl.edu/mowihsp/articles/practitioner.htm (Accessed 1/22/2016)).

66 Morris Fishbein, *A History of the American Medical Association, 1847 to 1947* (Philadelphia: W. B. Saunders, 1947), p. 19.

67 What Are the Oldest Medical Schools in the U.S.? http://www.answers.com/Q/What_are_the_Oldest_medical_schools_in_the_U.S. - slide1 (Accessed 11/3/2013).

68 University of Pennsylvania University Archives and Records Center, "University History—School of Medicine: A Brief History," http://www.archives.upenn.edu/histy/features/schools/med.html (Accessed 11/3/2013).

69 Harvard Medical School. "The History of HMS," http://hms.harvard.edu/about-hms/

history-hms (Accessed 11/3/2013).

70 Geisel School of Medicine at Dartmouth, "About the Geisel School of Medicine at Dartmouth," http://geiselmed.dartmouth.edu/about/ (Accessed 10/3/2013).

71 HealthCare 2.0, "History of Western Medicine," *http://bit.ly/1jw1HPr* (Accessed 12/6/2013).

72 Johns Hopkins Medicine, "The Four Founding Physicians," *http://www.hopkinsmedicine. org/about/history/history5.html* (Accessed 4/2/2013).

73 MedlinePlus, "Doctor of Medicine Profession (MD)," http://www.nlm.nih.gov/medlineplus/ency/article/001936.htm (Accessed 1/22/2013).

74 Adapted from an essay by his grandson, Nathan Smith Davis III, M.D., "Nathan Smith Davis, M.D., A.M., LL.D.," in Fishbein, *History of The American Medical Association*, pp. 3–16.

75 Ibid., p. 7

76 BMA: Who We Are: "The History of the BMA," http://bma.org.uk/about-the-bma/our-history (Accessed 3/22/2015).

77 Northwestern University, Feinberg School of Medicine. "Who Was Dr. Nathan Smith Davis?" http://www.feinberg.northwestern.edu/annualgivingreport/2013/about-nsd.html (Accessed 11/05/2014).

78 Fishbein, *History of the American Medical Association, pp. 60-61*

79 See Matthew Herper, "The Truly Staggering Cost of Inventing New Drugs," http://www.forbes.com/sites/matthewherper/2012/02/10/the-truly-staggering-cost-of-inventing-new-drugs/#6fe480434477 *Forbes*, February 10, 2012 (Accessed 11/5/2013).

80 Fishbein, *History of the American Medical Association*, p. 11.

81 Ibid., p. 109

82 Ibid., p. 112.

83 Texas Heart Institute at St. Luke's Episcopal Hospital: Continuing Medical Education, "Austin Flint," http://www.texasheart.org/Education/CME/explore/events/HSPS_austin_flint.cfm (Accessed 11/6/2013).

84 Fishbein, *History of the American Medical Association, p. 14*

85 Ibid., p. 35.

86 American Medical Association: Council on Ethical and Judicial Affairs, *Code of Medical Ethics: Current Opinions with Annotations* (AMA Press, 2004).

87 Fishbein, *History of the American Medical Association, p. 39.*

88 Kenneth A. Fisher and Lee S. Gross, "Fisher and Gross: Prudence of a Patient-Centered Approach; Allowing Patients to Choose Level of Care Would Result in Savings," *Washington Times*, May 3, 2012; accessible at: http://bit.ly/KyRqOc.

89 J. C. Mohr, *Licensed to Practice: The Supreme Court Defines the American Medical Profession* (Baltimore, MD: Johns Hopkins University Press, 2013), pp. 17-18.

90 Morris Fishbein, *A History of the American Medical Association, 1847 to 1947* (Philadelphia: W. B. Saunders, 1947), pp. 1010, 1012.

91 Mohr, *Licensed to Practice.* pp. 109-152

92 Ibid, p. 31.

93 Ibid, p. 91.

94 See http://doctorschar.com/archives/eclectic-school-of-medicine/.

95 U. S. Constitution, 14th Amendment, Section 1, available at, https://www.law.cornell.edu/constitution/amendmentxiv (Accessed 1/22/2016).

96 Fishbein, *History of the American Medical Association*, pp. 1017-18.

97 See the National Board of Medical Examiners site, at: http://www.nbme.org/about/index.html (Accessed 1/17/2014).

98 Kenneth M. Ludmerer, *Time to Heal: American Medical Education from the Turn of the Century to the Era of Managed Care* (New York: Oxford University Press, 1999), pp. 197-98.

99 National Board of Medical Examiners, http://www.nbme.org/about/index.html.

100 J. K. Iglehart and R. B. Baron, "Ensuring Physicians' Competence: Is Maintenance of Certification the Answer?" *New England Journal of Medicine* 367, 26: 2543-49.

101 J. C. Goodman, *Priceless: Curing Our Health Care Crisis,* chap. 5: "Why Do We Spend So Much on Healthcare?" (Oakland, CA: The Independent Institute, 2012), pp. 67-94.

102 Iglehart and Baron, "Ensuring Physicians' Competence," p. 2543.

103 Gray BM, Vandergrift JL, Johnston MM, Reschovsky JD, Lynn LA, Holmboe ES, McCullough JS, Lipner RS. Association Between Imposition of a Maintenance of Certification Requirement and Ambulatory Care–Sensitive Hospitalizations and Health Care Costs. JAMA. 2014;312(22):2348-2357. doi:10.1001/jama.2014.12716.

104 P. M. Kempen, "Maintenance of Certification Must Go: One Physician's Viewpoint," *Medical Economics,* January 23, 2014, http://bit.ly/1aYhy5Y. (Accessed 1/27/2014).

105 Jennifer Fong Ha and Nancy Longnecker, "Doctor-Patient Communication: A Review," *Ochsner Journal* 10, 1 (Spring 2010): 38-43.

106 Kurt Eichenwald, "The Ugly Civil War in American Medicine," *Newsweek* March 10, 2015, http://www.newsweek.com/2015/03/27/ugly-civil-war-american-medicine-312662.html (Accessed 3/27/2015).

107 You Tube, Dr. Josh Umber, Atlas MD, Wichita, KS, available at, https://www.youtube.com/watch?v=-PefZ7jpdr8 (Accessed 1/20/2016).

108 "AtlasMD", http://atlas.md/wichita/about-us/ (Accessed 3/28/2015).

109 "epiphany health", https://www.facebook.com/EpiphanyDPC/ (Accessed 1/22/2016).

110 NIHCM Foundation Data Brief, "The Concentration of Health Care Spending," July 2012, http://www.nihcm.org/pdf/DataBrief3%20Final.pdf (Accessed 4/3/2015).

111 Morris Fishbein, *A History of the American Medical Association, 1847 to 1947* (Philadelphia: W. B. Saunders, 1947), p. 201.

112 J. Duffy, *From Humors to Medical Science: A History of American Medicine,* 2nd ed. (Urbana, University of Illinois Press, 1993), pp. 223–24.

113 Encyclopedia.com, "American Medical Association," http://bit.ly/1hNhwSz (Accessed 12/18/2013).

114 Fishbein, *History of the American Medical Association,* pp. 205-213.

115 Ibid.

116 The AMA was initially incorporated in Illinois in 1897. Morris Fishbein, *A History of the American Medical Association, 1847 to 1947* (Philadelphia: W. B. Saunders, 1947), p. 835.

117 American Medical Association, "House of Delegates," http://www.ama-assn.org/ama/pub/about-ama/our-people/house-delegates.page (Accessed 12/04/2013).

118 American Medical Association, "Member Organizations," http://www.ama-assn.org/ama/pub/about-ama/our-people/house-delegates/the-delegates/member-organizations.page? (Accessed 12/04/2013).

119 American Medical Association, "The Delegates," http://www.ama-assn.org/ama/pub/about-ama/our-people/house-delegates/the-delegates.page? (Accessed 12/5/2013).

120 Fishbein, *History of the American Medical Association,* p. 204.

121 Ibid., pp. 203-4, 1019.

122 John Duffy, *From Humors to Medical Science: A History of American Medicine,* 2nd ed. (Urbana: University of Illinois Press, 1993), pp. 203-4.

123 Ibid., pp. 204-5.

124 Ibid., p. 205.

125 Fishbein, *History of the American Medical Association,* p. 889.

126 Duffy, *From Humors to Medical* Science, p. 209.

127 American Association of Medical Colleges. *Women in Academic Medicine Statistics and Medical School Benchmarking, 2011-2012: Medical Students, Selected Years, 1965-2012,* https://www.aamc.org/download/305282/data/2012_table1.pdf (Accessed 2/16/2014).

128 Arthur Dean Bevan, "Report of the Committee on Medical Education," *JAMA* 40: 1,372 (May 16, 1903).

129 Fishbein, *History of the American Medical Association*, p. 887.

130 "State Board Statistics for 1907," *JAMA* 50: 184 (May 30, 1908).

131 "Third Annual Congress on Medical Education," *JAMA* 48: 1,701 (May 18, 1907).

132 Abraham Flexner, *Medical Education in the United States and Canada: A Report to the Carnegie Foundation for the Advancement of Teaching* (Boston: D. B. Updike, Merrymount Press), 1910.

133 Fishbein, *History of the American Medical Association*, p. 902.

134 P. J. Seward, *Caring for the Country: A History and Celebration of the First 150 Years of the American Medical Association* (Chicago: American Medical Association, 1997), p. 54.

135 Ibid., p. 73.

136 Graduates of Canadian medical schools are not considered foreign medical graduates.

137 AAMC (Association of American Medical Colleges), "Medical School Applicants, Enrollment Reach All-Time Highs," *http://bit.ly/1dS28Ss* (Accessed 2/20/2014).

138 Duffy, *From Humors to Medical* Science, p. 279.

139 Kenneth A. Fisher with Lindsay E. Rockwell and Missy Scott, *In Defiance of Death: Exposing the Real Costs of End-of-Life Care* (Westport, CT: Praeger, 2008).

140 Marian Wilde, "Global Grade: How Do U.S. Students Compare?" (Great Schools), *http://bit.ly/1kX8wM7* (Accessed 2/19/2014).

141 Anne Underwood (interviewing Prof. Uwe E. Reinhardt), *Prescriptions:* "Health Care Abroad: Germany," *New York Times*, September 29, 2009, http://prescriptions.blogs. nytimes.com/2009/09/29/health-care-abroad-germany/?_php=true&_type=blogs&_r=0.

142 The National Archives [UK], The Cabinet Papers, 1915-1984: "National Health Insurance: National Health Insurance Act 1911," https://www.nationalarchives.gov.uk/cabinetpapers/themes/national-health-insurance.htm (Accessed 4/2/2014).

143 John Duffy, *From Humors to Medical Science: A History of American Medicine*, 2nd ed. (Urbana, University of Illinois Press, 1993), p. 318.

144 Morris Fishbein, *A History of the American Medical Association, 1847 To 1947*, (Philadelphia: W. B. Saunders, 1947).

145 Ibid., pp. 286-87.

146 Ibid., p. 292

147 Ibid., pp. 292-93, 296-98.

148 Ibid., pp. 320-21.

149 Duffy, *From Humors to Medical Science*, p. 319.

150 Fishbein, *History of the American Medical Association*, p. 331

151 Ibid., p. 329.

152 Jone Johnson Lewis, "Sheppard-Towner Act of 1921," About.Com, About Education, Women's History, *http://womenshistory.about.com/od/laws/a/sheppard-towner. htm?p=1* (Accessed 4/4/2014).

153 Infoplease, "America's Wars: U.S. Casualties and Veterans," *http://www.infoplease.com/ ipa/A0004615.html* (Accessed 4/6/2014).

154 Encyclopedia of Chicago, "Veterans' Hospitals," http://bit.ly/1mPhTvJ (Accessed 4/6/2014).

155 Department of Veterans Affairs, "VA History In Brief," http://www.va.gov/opa/publications/archives/docs/history_in_brief.pdf (Accessed 4/6/2014).

156 Encyclopedia of Chicago, "Veterans' Hospitals."

157 Fishbein, *History of the American Medical Association*, pp. 336, 482.

158 Duffy, *From Humors to Medical Science*, p. 319.

159 Fishbein, *History of the American Medical Association*, p. 399.

160 Wellmark Blue Cross and Blue Shield, "History," http://bit.ly/1g3OSv3 (Accessed 4/8/2014).

161 Marc Lichtenstein, Blue Cross and Blue Shield blog: "Health Insurance from Invention to Innovation: A History of the Blue Cross and Blue Shield Companies," *http://bit.ly/1iucFTl* (Accessed 4/8/2014).

162 Wellmark Blue Cross and Blue Shield, "History."

163 Fishbein, *History of the American Medical Association*, p. 385.

164 Ibid., p. 958.

165 John P. Seward, *Caring for the Country: A History and Celebration of the First 150 Years of the American Medical Association* (Chicago, American Medical Association, 1997), p. 48.

166 Social Security Administration, " Edwin E. Witte (1887-1960):, Father of Social Security" (Wilbur J. Cohen), http://www.ssa.gov/history/cohenwitte.html (Accessed 4/10/2014).

167 Fishbein, *History of the American Medical Association*, pp. 413-14.

168 Ibid., pp. 415-16.

169 Ibid., p. 418.

170 Social Security Administration, "The Social Security Act of 1935," http://www.ssa.gov/history/35act.html (Accessed 4/11/2014).

171 Seward, *Caring for the Country*, p. 53.

172 Frank D. Campion, *The AMA and U.S. Health Policy since 1940* (Chicago, Chicago Review Press, 1984), pp. 128-31.

173 Leo J. Linder and Morris A. Wainger, "The Wagner-Murray-Dingell Social Security Bill of 1945: A Social Security Charter for Peacetime America," HeinOnline. http://bit.ly/1tjGNbe.

174 Campion, *The AMA and U.S. Health Policy since* 1940, p. 138.

175 Kathleen Doherty and Jeffery A. Jenkins "Examining a Failed Moment: National Health Care, the AMA, and the U.S. Congress, 1948-50" (January 7, 2009; paper prepared for presentation at the 2009 Annual Meeting of the Southern Political Science Association, New Orleans, LA), available at http://faculty.virginia.edu/jajenkins/health_care.pdf (Accessed 4/14/2014).

176 Odin W. Anderson, *Blue Cross since 1929: Accountability and the Public Trust* (Cambridge, MA: Ballinger, 1975), p. 62.

177 "Why did Truman win the presidential election of 1948? Why was his victory considered a major upset?" Yahoo Answers, *http://yhoo.it/1r7NZ6j.*

178 Senator Lester Hill (D-AL) & Senator George Aiken (R-VT).

179 Campion, *The AMA and U.S. Health Policy since* 1940, p. 165.

180 Doherty and Jenkins, "Examining a Failed Moment," pp. 7-12.

181 Ibid., pp. 16-19.

182 Rick Mayes. *Universal Coverage: The Elusive Quest for National Health Insurance*, (Ann Arbor, University of Michigan Press, 2004) pp. 62-64.

183 Campion, *The AMA and U.S. Health Policy since* 1940, p. 254.

184 Ibid., pp. 260-67.

185 Frank D. Campion *The AMA and U.S. Health Policy: Since 1940* (Chicago: Chicago Review Press, 1984), p. 269.

186 Campion, *The AMA and U.S. Health Policy*, p. 270.

187 Just imagine what healthcare would look like today if the liberal group had held sway at that time.

188 Ibid., p. 271.

189 Cronkite Walter, "The Landslide Election of 1964" (*All Things Considered*—Walter Cronkite: History's Lessons), National Public Radio, November 2, 2004, *http://n.pr/1nBrGsM.* (Accessed 5/12/2014).

190 Theodore R. Marmor, *The Politics of Medicare*, Hawthorne New York, U.S.A. : Aldine Transaction, 2000, p. 56.

191 "AMA House Backs Eldercare Program, Asks Study of Kerr-Mills Expansion," *JAMA* 191 (8):32-33 (1965), available at http://jama.jamanetwork.com/article.aspx?articleid=654978. (Accessed 7/8/2014).

192 *Proceedings of the AMA House of Delegates,* February 6-7, 1965, p. 19.

193 Campion, *The AMA and U.S. Health Policy,* p. 276.

194 Personal communications with Dr. Russell B. Roth, August, 1979, and Wilbur J. Cohen, February, 1980, both present at the meeting, which was conducted by Frank D. Campion.

195 Campion, *The AMA and U.S. Health Policy,* pp. 280-81.

196 Frédéric Bastiat, "What Is Seen and What Is Not Seen" (Library of Economics and Liberty: *Selected Essays on Political Economy*), http://bit.ly/1mZ0cJK. (Accessed5/14/2014).

197 Charles E. Phelps, "Public Sector Medicine: History and Analysis," in *New Directions in Public Health Care,* ed. C. M. Lindsay (San Francisco: Institute for Contemporary Studies, 1976), pp. 135-36.

198 Avik Roy. "Saving Medicare from Itself," *National Affairs* (Summer 2011), pp. 40-41, http://www.nationalaffairs.com/doclib/20110623_Roy.pdf. (Accessed 5/13/2014).

199 Avik, "Saving Medicare from Itself," pp. 39-40.

200 Brandon D. Bushnell, American Academy of Orthopaedic Surgeons, "The Evolution of DRGs," *http://bit.ly/1p0qU62.* (Accessed 5/18/2014).

201 Avik, "Saving Medicare from Itself," p. 43.

202 Michael Grunwald. "How to Cut Health Care Costs: Less Care, More Data," *Time,* June 29, 2009.

203 Christina Romer and Mark Duggan, "Exploring the Link between Rising Health Insurance Premiums and Stagnant Wages," White House, Council of Economic Advisers, March 12, 2010, http://1.usa.gov/VsDfa0. (Accessed 7/5/2014).

204 Keith Smith, "What a Scorpion Sting Teaches Us about Hospitals and Insurance," Association of American Physicians and Surgeons, September 13, 2012, http://bit.ly/1lwOnJN. (Accessed 8/15/2014).

205 Roni Caryn Rabin, "Well: The Confusion of Hospital Pricing," *New York Times,* April 23, 2012, http://nyti.ms/1oBuyWJ. (5/17/2014).

206 Holman W. Jenkins, Jr., "Yes, Hospital Pricing Is Insane, But Why?" *Wall Street Journal,* March 1, 2013, http://on.wsj.com/1ra3HmH. (Accessed 3/27/2014).

207 Department of Health and Human Services, Centers for Medicare & Medicaid Services, Medicare Learning Network, "Acute Care Hospital Inpatient Prospective Payment System: Payment System Fact Sheet Series," April 2013, http://go.cms.gov/1oB5tsO. (5/26/2014).

208 Milton Friedman, "Economics of Socialized Medicine" (Mayo Clinic, 1978), http://www.youtube.com/watch?v=VPADFNKDhGM&list=PL39A572EB77914E00&index=2. (Accessed 12/22/2012).

209 G. J. Bazzoli, A. Gerland, and J. May, "Construction Activity in U.S. Hospitals: The Financial Impact of Existing Construction Activity on Consumers and Health Plans Is Likely to Be Substantial," *Health Affairs* 25:3 (May-June 2006), 783-91.

210 "Doctors-In-Training Spend Very Little Time at Patient Bedside, Study Finds" (Johns Hopkins Medicine: News and Publications, April 23, 2013), http://bit.ly/1tA4klv. (Accessed 5/20/2014).

211 Avik, "Saving Medicare from Itself," p. 45.

212 Louis Jacobson, "Barbara Boxer Says Medicare Overhead Is Far Lower Than Private Insurers' Overhead," *Tampa Bay Times,* May 30, 2011, http://bit.ly/S9Brkd. (Accessed 5/26/2014).

213 Federal Register: Daily Journal of the United States Government, Health Care Finance Administration, http://1.usa.gov/1ilZG5k. (Accessed 5/26/2014).

214 William G. Schiffbauer. "The Level Playing Field Myth: Comparing Administrative

Costs for Public, Private Health Insurance" (BNA's Medicare Report), April 24, 2009, http://bit.ly/1nVbwXL. (Accessed 5/28/2014).

215 Avik, "Saving Medicare from Itself," pp. 35, 45.

216 Ibid., p. 40.

217 Susan Jaffe, "The New Health Care Law and Annual and Lifetime Coverage Limits" (AARP Bulletin, August 23, 2010), http://bit.ly/1o8XhyJ. (Accessed 5/31/2014).

218 American College of Emergency Physicians: Clinical & Practice Management, "RBRVS FAQ" (Last updated 06/2014), http://www.acep.org/Clinical---Practice-Management/RBRVS-FAQ/. (5/30/2014).

219 Ibid.

220 Kent J. Moore, Thomas A. Felger, Walter L. Larimore, and Terry L. Mills, Jr., "What Every Physician Should Know about the RUC," *Family Practice Management* 15:2 (February 2008), 36-39, http://www.aafp.org/fpm/2008/0200/p36.html. (6/1/2014).

221 Phillips Gausewitz, "Why Medical Price Controls Are a Terrible Idea," *The Federalist* (April 25, 2014), http://bit.ly/1mRpla1. (Accessed 5/1/2014).

222 Reason.tv, "How to Fix Health Care: Lasik Surgery for the Medical Debate," Reason. com. Hit & Run Blog, December 2, 2009, http://bit.ly/1ojmQ0c. (6/1/2014).

223 "Doctors Expose AMA's Secret Pact with Federal Government: Applaud Sen. Lott's Challenge of AMA Monopoly" (AAPS press release, August 8, 2001), http://bit.ly/1mGQiMu. (Accessed 6/1/2014).

224 Jeff Pilato, "Charging vs. Coding: Untangling the Relationship for ICD-10," *Journal of AHIMA* 84, no. 2 (February 2013): 58-60, http://bit.ly/1rU0LKt. (7/8/2014).

225 Department of Health and Human Services, "2013 Actuarial Report on the Financial Outlook for Medicaid," http://www.medicaid.gov/Medicaid-CHIP-Program-Information/By-Topics/Financing-and-Reimbursement/Downloads/medicaid-actuarial-report-2013.pdf. (Accessed 5/30/2014).

226 Julia Bienstock, "Administrative Oversight of State Medicaid Payment Policies: Giving Teeth to the Equal Access Provision" (2013), http://bit.ly/1l6zfFe. (Accessed 5/31/2014).

227 Vee Burke, "The 1996 Welfare Reform Law" (Congressional Research Service, Welfare Reform Briefing Book), http://royce.house.gov/uploadedfiles/the%201996%20welfare%20reform%20law.pdf (6/6/2014).

228 Statista—The Statistics Portal, "Total Medicaid Enrollment from 1966 to 2014 (in millions)," http://bit.ly/1hldeDd. (Accessed 6/6/2014).

229 Texas State Library and Archives Commission, "United States and Texas Populations 1850-2012," http://bit.ly/1hEkbQe. (Accessed 6/6/2014).

230 Bienstock, "Administrative Oversight of State Medicaid Payment Policies," p. 5.

231 U.S. Social Security Administration, Office of Retirement and Disability Policy (Annual Statistical Supplement, 2011), "Medicaid Program Description and Legislative History," http://www.ssa.gov/policy/docs/statcomps/supplement/2011/medicaid.html. (Accessed 6/1/2014).

232 Statista—The Statistics Portal, "Total Medicaid Federal & State Expenditures in the United States from 1966 to 2014 (in billion U.S. dollars)," http://www.statista.com/statistics/245350/total-medicaid-federal-and-state-expenditure-in-the-us-since-1966/. (Accessed 6/6/2014).

233 Statista—The Statistics Portal, "Projected Total Medicaid Federal and State Expenditures from 2015 to 2022 (in billion U.S. dollars)," http://www.statista.com/statistics/245452/projected-total-medicaid-federal-and-state-expenditures/. (Accessed 6/6/2014).

234 $ Dollar Times, "Inflation Calculator: The Changing Value of a Dollar," *http://www.dollartimes.com/calculators/inflation.htm.* (Accessed 7/8/2014)

235 Phil Galewitz, "A Dozen States Slice Medicaid Payments to Doctors, Hospitals" (Kaiser Health News, July 6, 2011), http://bit.ly/1kIgubH. (Accessed 6/7/2014).

236 42 U.S.C. 139a(a)(30)(A) (2006).

237 Bienstock, "Administrative Oversight of State Medicaid Payment Policies," p. 11.

238."US Supreme Court Defers a Decision on the Douglas Medicaid Cases: Provider and Beneficiary Challenges to Medicaid Payment Reductions Still in Question," Dentons, February 23, 2012, http://bit.ly/1kT4Ieh. (Accessed 6/1/2014

239 Joanna Bisgaier and Karin V. Rhodes, "Auditing Access to Specialty Care for Children with Public Insurance," *New England Journal of Medicine* 364 (June 16, 2011): 2324-33.

240 John C. Goodman, "How Will Obamacare Affect Medicare Patients?" *(*February 6, 2013), https://www.psychologytoday.com/blog/curing-the-healthcare-crisis/201302/how-will-obamacare-affect-medicare-patients. (Accessed6/8/2014).

241 Rebecca Voelker, "Emergency Visits Up in Massachusetts after Reforms Enacted" (March 20, 2014), http://newsatjama.jama.com/2014/03/20/emergency-visits-up-in-massachusetts-after-reforms-enacted/. (Accessed 6/9/2014).

242 Sarah L. Taubman, Heidi L. Allen, Bill J. Wright, Katherine Baicker, and Amy N. Finkelstein, "Medicaid Increases Emergency-Department Use: Evidence from Oregon's Health Insurance Experiment," *Science* 343 (January 17, 2014): 263-68, http://www.sciencemag.org/content/343/6168/263.abstract. (Accessed 6/6/2014).

243 Katherine Baicker, Sarah L. Taubman, Heidi L. Allen, Mira Bernstein, Jonathan H. Gruber, Joseph P. Newhouse, Eric C. Schneider, Bill J. Wright, Alan M. Zaslavsky, and Amy N. Finkelstein, "The Oregon Experiment: Effects of Medicaid on Clinical Outcomes," *New England Journal of Medicine* 368 (2013): 1713-22.

244 Ibid., The Oregon study revealed that with Medicaid as insurance, there was no improvement in patients with serious chronic medical conditions.

245 Seth A. Watts, Bradley N. Reames, Kyle H. Sheetz, Michael J. Englesbe, and Darrell A. Cambell, Jr., "Anticipating the Effects of Medicaid Expansion on Surgical Care," *JAMA Surg.* 149 (July 2014): 745-47, http://archsurg.jamanetwork.com/article.aspx?articleid=1867405. (Accessed 6/8/2014).

246 Avik Roy, "UVa Study: Surgical Patients on Medicaid Are 13% More Likely to Die Than Those without Insurance," July 27, 2010, http://www.nationalreview.com/article/313120/medicaid-americas-worst-health-care-program-avik-roy (Accessed 6/10/2014).

247 Avik Roy, "Why Medicaid Is a Humanitarian Catastrophe," Forbes: The Apothecary, March 2, 2011, available at: http://www.forbes.com/sites/theapothecary/2011/03/02/why-medicaid-is-a-humanitarian-catastrophe/ (Accessed 6/11/2014).

248 Avik Roy, "Obama Administration Denies Waiver for Indiana's Popular Medicaid Program," Forbes: The Apothecary, November 11, 2011, http://www.forbes.com/sites/aroy/2011/11/11/obama-administration-denies-waiver-for-indianas-popular-medicaid-reform/ (Accessed 5/15/2014).

249 "Healthy Indiana Plan: Frequently Asked Questions; Eligibility," http://bit.ly/1lVg9OA. (Accessed 7/9/2014).

250 Greg Scandlen, "New RAND Study of Consumer-Directed Health Plans" (National Center for Policy Analysis: Health Policy Blog, June 17, 2011), http://healthblog.ncpa.org/new-rand-study-of-consumer-directed-health-plans/. (Accessed 6/11/2014).

251 Avik Roy, *How Medicaid Fails the Poor* (New York: Encounter Books, 2013), p. 37.

252 Epiphany Health, available at, http://socialsquare.wix.com/epiphany-health (Accessed 1/22/2016).

253 "Estimated Sustainable Growth Rate and Conversion Factor, for Medicare Payments to Physicians in 2015", available on line at, https://www.cms.gov/medicare/medicare-fee-for-service-payment/sustainablegratesconfact/downloads/sgr2015p.pdf (Accessed 1/22/2016).

254 Ken Fisher, MD. *Congress Continues Down The Yellow Brick Fantasy Road With MACRA*, Medical Economics, October 29, 2016, available at: http://buff.ly/2dUnuBK (Accessed October 29, 2016)

255 American College of Emergency Physicians: Clinical & Practice Management, "RBRVS FAQ" (Last updated 06/2014), http://www.acep.org/Clinical---Practice-Management/RBRVS-FAQ/. (Accessed 5/30/2014).

256 Mimi Bernardin, Julie A. Schoenman, Internet Archive, Final Report, "Analysis of Inappropriate Utilization and Lack of Access for the Purpose of Determining the Medicare Volume Performance Standards," April 10, 1991, available at: http://bit.ly/WPJIwT. (Accessed 7/30/2014).

257 Committee on Finance, Calendar No. 280, 113th Congress, 2nd Session, *Report 113-135*.

258 American Osteopathic Association, Issue Brief, "Background: How Physicians Are Paid Under Medicare," available at: http://www.osteopathic.org/inside-aoa/public-policy/regulatory-issues/Documents/sgr-how-physicians-are-paid-medicare.pdf. (Accessed 4/224/2015).

259 "Estimated Sustainable Growth Rate and Conversion Factor, for Medicare Payments to Physicians in 2015" Ibid.

260 "Sustainable Growth Rate (SGR): Summary," http://www.acponline.org/advocacy/state_health_policy/hottopics/sgr.pdf. (Accessed 7/28/2014).

261 Bob Doherty, "*10 Reasons to Like the Bills That Repeal the SGR*" (December 26, 2013), http://www.kevinmd.com/blog/2013/12/10-reasons-bills-repeal-sgr.html. (Accessed 6/25/2014).

262 Stuart Guterman, "The "Doc Fix":- Another Missed Opportunity," *New England Journal of Medicine*; 370 (2014): 2261-63.

263 "H.R.2 Medicare Access And Chip Reauthorization Act, Section by Section," available at: http://energycommerce.house.gov/sites/republicans.energycommerce.house.gov/files/114/Analysis/20150324-HR2-SectionbySection.pdf (Accessed 4/25/2015).

264 Kurt Eichenwald, "A Certified Medical Controversy," *Newsweek* (4/7/2015), available at: http://www.newsweek.com/certified-medical-controversy-320495 (Accessed 4/25/2015).

265 John R. Graham, National Center For Policy Analysis, "Fix The Flawed Medicare Doc Fix," (April 2015), http://www.ncpa.org/pdfs/st364.pdf (Accessed 4/22/2015).

266 Margaret Rose, Tech Target, "HITECH Act (Health Information Technology for Economic and Clinical Health Act) Definition", available on line at, http://searchhealthit.techtarget.com/definition/HITECH-Act (Accessed 1/22/2016).

267 Reed Abelson and Julie Creswell, "In Second Look, Few Savings from Digital Health Records," *New York Times*, January 10, 2013, available at: http://nyti.ms/1ywW7kD. (8/13/2014).

268 The White House, "Remarks by the President and Vice President at Signing of the American Recovery and Reinvestment Act", February 17, 2009 available online at, https://www.whitehouse.gov/the-press-office/remarks-president-and-vice-president-signing-american-recovery-and-reinvestment-act (Accessed 1/22/2016).

269 Christopher Rowland, Globe Staff, "Hazards tied to medical records push: Subsidies given for computerizing, but no reporting required when errors cause harm", July 20, 2014, available online at, http://bit.ly/1nr4fFj (Accessed 1/22/2016).

270 CMS.gov, "Physician Quality Reporting System," (May, 01, 2015), available at: http://www.cms.gov/Medicare/Quality-Initiatives-Patient-Assessment-Instruments/PQRS/ (Accessed 5/6/2015).

271 HealthIT.gov, "EHR Incentives & Certification", available online at, https://www.healthit.gov/providers-professionals/ehr-incentive-programs (Accessed 1/22/2016).

272 Nir Menachemi and Taleah H. Collum, "Benefits and Drawbacks of Electronic Health Record Systems," *Risk Management and Healthcare Policy* 4 (2011): 47-55, available at: http://www.ncbi.nlm.nih.gov/pmc/articles/PMC3270933/ (Accessed 8/14/2014).

273 Jeffrey Powalisz. "Certified EHR Technology" (EHR Intelligence, April 25, 2012), http://bit.ly/1pOljBh (Accessed 8/13/2014).

274 Kyle Murphy, "What Does the RAND Study Really Say about EHR Adoption, Cost Savings?" (EHR Intelligence, January 18, 2013), http://bit.ly/1kzZwhk (Accessed 8/12/2014).

275 CMS, "Medicare & Medicaid HER Incentive Program: Meaningful Use Stage 1 Requirements Overview", 2010, available online at, https://www.cms.gov/Regulations-and-Guidance/Legislation/EHRIncentivePrograms/downloads/MU_Stage1_ReqOverview.pdf (Accessed 1/23/2016).

276 Many core and menu objectives include information that would be part of any standard history or physical exam; as such, they should not need separate documentation. See Group One Healthsource, MU Certified eClinical Works EHR Demo, available at: http://bit.ly/1GJa1qy (Accessed 11/10/2014).

277 HRSA, "Meaningful Use Stage 2", available online, http://www.hrsa.gov/healthit/meaningfuluse/stage2/ (Accessed 1/23/2016).

278 Kyle Murphy, "AHA, AMA, CHIME Challenge Stage 3 Meaningful Use Proposals" (EHR Intelligence, January 16, 2013), http://bit.ly/1rsicxX (Accessed 8/13/2014).

279 CMS.gov, Centers for Medicare & Medicaid Services, "Medicare and Medicaid EHR Incentive Program Basics," http://go.cms.gov/1ir7M1Z (Accessed 8/14/2014).

280 Anna Wilde Mathews. "Same Doctor Visit, Double the Cost: Insurers Say Rates Can Surge after Hospitals Buy Private Physician Practices; Medicare Spending Rises, Too," *Wall Street Journal*, August 27,2012, available at: http://on.wsj.com/1o35TFf (Accessed 8/14/2014).

281 Menachemi and Collum, "Benefits and Drawbacks of Electronic Health Record Systems," pp. 2-4.

282 Ibid., pp. 1-12.

283 Edward Volpintesta, "Administrative Overload as a Cause of Diagnostic Error," *JAMA Internal Medicine* 173: 1927 (2013).

284 Joyce Frieden, "Misdiagnosis: Can It Be Remedied?" MEDPAGE TODAY, August 15, 2014, http://bit.ly/1rFUMp9 (Accessed 8/16/2014).

285 David E. Newman-Toker and Martin A. Makary, "Measuring Diagnostic Errors in Primary Care: The First Step on a Path Forward; Comment on 'Types and Origins of Diagnostic Errors in Primary Care Settings,'" *JAMA Internal Medicine* 173: 425-26 (2013).

286 Reed and Creswell, "In Second Look."

287 Daniel R. Verdon, Physician Outcry on EHR Functionality, Cost Will Shake the Health Information Technology Sector, *Medical Economics*, February 10, 2014, available at: http://bit.l/NsYODH. (Accessed 8/18/2014).

288 Pamela Hartzband and Jerome Groopman, "Off the Record: Avoiding the Pitfalls of Going Electronic," *New England Journal of Medicine* 358: 1656-58 (2008).

289 Lauren Block, "Doctors-In-Training Spend Very Little Time at Patient Bedside, Study Finds: Time with Patients Seems "Squeezed Out" of Training, Investigator Says," Johns Hopkins Medicine—News and Publications, April 23, 2013, available at: http://bit.ly/1tA4klv. (5/20/2013).

290 K. Patrick Ober, William B. Applegate, "The electronic record: Are we tools of our tools?" *The Pharos*, Winter 2015, available at: http://alphaomegaalpha.org/pharos/PDFs/2015-1-Ober-Applegate.pdf (Accessed 5/4/2015).

291 Jeffrey Young, "Employee Health Insurance Costs Barely Increased This Year," Huff Post (September, 10, 2014), available at: http://www.huffingtonpost.com/2014/09/10/employee-health-insurance_n_5787292.html (Accessed 5/5/2015).

292 Daily KOS, "Will the HITECH Act and EHR's inadvertently lead to the demise of Primary Care in America? (August 17,2014), available at: http://www.dailykos.com/story/2014/08/17/1317104/-Will-the-HITECH-Act-and-EHR-s-inadvertently-lead-to-the-demise-of-primary-medical-care-in-America# (Accessed 5/8/2015).

293 Jason Fodeman, "The New Health Law: Bad For Doctors, Awful For Patients," The

Institute for Health Care Consumerism (2015), available at: http://www.theihcc.com/en/ communities/policy_legislation/the-new-health-law-bad-for-doctors-awful-for-patie_ gn17y01k.html (Accessed 5/8/2015).

294 Abraham Fuks, James Brawer, and J. Donald Boudreau, "The Foundation of Physician-ship," *Perspectives in Biology and Medicine* 55:114-26 (2012).

295 Meg Edison, "Confessions of a Narrow Network Doctor," *Rebel.MD* (August 19, 2014), available at: http://rebel.md/confessions-of-a-narrow-network-doctor/ (Accessed 1/23/2016).

296 Uwe Reinhardt, "You Think Financing U.S. Health Care Is Bizarre? Check Out 340B Drug Pricing," *Forbes—The Apothecary* (August 21, 2014), available at: http://onforb.es/ XDDbFV. (Accessed 8/22/2014).

297 "Summary of the Affordable Care Act" (Henry J. Kaiser Family Foundation), April 25, 2013), available at: http://kff.org/health-reform/fact-sheet/summary-of-the-affordable-care-act/ (Accessed 8/27/2014).

298 "Remarks of President Barack Obama—Address to Joint Session of Congress," February 24, 2009, available at: https://www.whitehouse.gov/video/EVR022409 - transcript.

299 Obamacare Facts, *Affordable Care Act Summary*, available at: http://obamacarefacts. com/affordablecareact-summary/ (Accessed 11/10/2014).

300 Jonathan Wu, "The Biggest Problem with the ACA Federal Exchange," http://www.val-uepenguin.com/2013/10/biggest-problem-federal-exchange (Accessed 8/31/2014).

301 United States Senate Committee on Finance, "Failed Obamacare State Exchanges, Bur-well, and a Bill to Fix It: A Closer Look at the Hundreds of Millions of Taxpayer Dollars Wasted" (May 16, 2014), available at: http://1.usa.gov/1k9cvUD. (Accessed 8.1/2014).

302 Michael F. Cannon, "Statement on D.C. Circuit's Ruling in Halbig v. Burwell" (CATO Institute: Cato at Liberty, July 22, 2014), available at: http://bit.ly/1nPRTzt (Accessed 8/1/2014).

303 Reps. John Kline, Paul Ryan and Fred Upton. "An Off-Ramp From ObamaCare: If the Supreme Court follow the law, there will be an opening for a sane health-care alterna-tive. Here it is." Wall Street Journal, March 2, 2015, available at: http://www.wsj.com/ar-ticles/paul-ryan-john-kline-and-fred-upton-an-off-ramp-from-obamacare-1425340840 (Accessed 5/6/2015).

304 Rep. Diane Black. "The Coming Obamacare Tax-Filing Nightmare," Forbes—The Apoth-ecary, August 27, 2014, available at: http://onforb.es/1vDm5pp (Accessed 8/28/2014).

305 Nigam Arora, "Insurance Agents Lose Job Security with Obamacare Ruling," Forbes, June 29, 2012, available at: http://onforb.es/1Ck9MA6 (Accessed 9/1/2014).

306 Louise B. Russell, "Preventing Chronic Disease: An Important Investment, But Don't Count on Cost Savings; An Overwhelming Percentage of Preventative Interventions Add More to Medical Costs Than They Save," *Health Affairs* 28:42-45 (2009). (PMID 19124852).

307 Val Jones, "Why False Positive Results Are So Common in Medicine," *Science-Based Medicine*, July 23, 2009, available online http://www.scienceinmedicine.org/fellows/ Jones.html scroll down to the actual article (Accessed 1/23/2016).

308 George J. Annas, Theodore W. Ruger, and Jennifer Prah Ruger. "Money, Sex, and Reli-gion: The Supreme Court's ACA Sequel," *New England Journal of Medicine* 371: 862-66 (2014) (PMID 25029337).

309 informed on reform, Essential Health Benefits, Fact Sheet, available at: http://www. cigna.com/assets/docs/about-cigna/informed-on-reform/cigna-essential-health-bene-fits-fact-sheet.pdf (Accessed 11/11/2014).

310 NCSL, "Mandated Health Insurance Benefits and State Laws: Updated & material added January 2014", available at, http://www.ncsl.org/research/health/mandated-health-insurance-benefits-and-state-laws.aspx (Accessed 1/23/2016).

311 Wall Street Journal, "Obamacare's $1,200 Pay Cut", January 12, 2016, available at, http://

www.wsj.com/articles/obamacares-1-200-pay-cut-1452643649 (Accessed 1/21/2016).

312 Raven Clabough, "ObamaCare and the President's Broken Promises," *New American*, November 22, 2013, available at: http://bit.ly/1sXLTYH (Accessed 9/2/2014).

313 CMS.gov, Centers for Medicare & Medicaid Services, "*Emergency Medical Treatment & Labor Act (EMTALA)*," March 26, 2012, available at: http://go.cms.gov/1CnI9X2 (Accessed 9/2/2014).

314 Stacey B.Rowland and Douglas S. Clark, Wilson Elser, "Navigators & Agents and Brokers: How They Fit into the Health Insurance Exchange Formula," May 6, 2013, available at: http://bit.ly/1pmyRAa (Accessed 9/2/2014).

315 "Health Expenditure Projections 2012-2022: Forecast Summary," available at: http://go.cms.gov/1jNw5Bk. (Accessed 8/15/2014).

316 John C. Goodman, "Is Obamacare Slowing Health Care Spending"? Forbes, December 4, 2014, available at: http://www.forbes.com/sites/johngoodman/2014/12/04/is-obamacare-slowing-health-care-spending/#242d50a449a9 (Accessed 1/23/2016).

317 Stephen T. Parente, "The Short Unhappy Life of ObamaCare," *Wall Street Journal*, June 10, 2014, available at: http://on.wsj.com/1nwXJaU. (Accessed 6/15/2014).

318 Kenneth J. Arrow, "Uncertainty and the Welfare Economics of Medical Care, "Bulletin of the World Health Organization (February 2004, 82 (2)), available at: http://www.who.int/bulletin/volumes/82/2/PHCBP.pdf (5/5/2015).

319 Ibid.

320 Avik J. A. Roy, "Liberals Are Wrong: Free Market Health Care Is Possible," The Atlantic, Business, Megan Mcardle, editor, (March 18, 2012) available at: http://www.theatlantic.com/business/archive/2012/03/liberals-are-wrong-free-market-health-care-is-possible/254648/ (Accessed 5/21/2015).

321 Ibid.

322 Fast Stats, CDC, "Health Expenditures," available at: http://www.cdc.gov/nchs/fastats/health-expenditures.htm (Accessed 5/24/2015).

323 Clare Krusing, AHIP, "New Census Survey Shows Continued Growth in HSA Enrollment," (July 9, 2014), available at: https://www.ahip.org/Press-Room/2014/HSA-Census-Survey/ (Accessed 5/22/2015).

324 Atul Gawande, "Overkill: An avalanche of unnecessary medical care is harming patients physically and financially. What can we do about it?, *The New Yorker* (May 11,2005), available at: http://www.newyorker.com/magazine/2015/05/11/overkill-atul-gawande (Accessed 5/19/2015).

325 David Goldhill, *Catastrophic Care: Why Everything We Know About Health Care Is Wrong* (New York: Vintage Books, Division of Random House, 2013) p. 200.

326 Alyene Senger, "Obamacare's Impact on Seniors: An Update" (Heritage Foundation, Issue Brief #4019 on Health Care, August 20, 2013), available at: http://herit.ag/WO7R5U (Accessed 9/11/2014).

327 Edie Littlefield Sundby, "You Also Can't Keep Your Doctor," *Wall Street Journal*, November 3, 2013, available at: http://on.wsj.com/1jpcj46. (Accessed 9/11/2014).

328 Health Savings Accounts (HSAs) were created in 2003 so that individuals covered by high-deductible health plans could receive tax-preferred treatment of money saved for medical expenses.

329 Merrill Matthews, "Health Savings Accounts Will Survive Obamacare—At Least for Now," *Forbes*, March 27, 2013, available at: http://onforb.es/1pcaZj2. (Accessed 9/11/2014).

330 Stephen C. Schimpff, KevinMD.com, "No Direct Primary Care Isn't Too Expensive," (August 25, 2014), available at: http://www.kevinmd.com/blog/2014/08/direct-primary-care-isnt-expensive.html (Accessed 5/11/2015).

331 Epiphany Health, http://socialsquare.wix.com/epiphany-health (Accessed 1/23/2016) and ATLAS MD, "We're Here for You. All the Time," available at: http://atlas.md/wichita

(Accessed 9/12/2014).

332 Daniel McCorry, "Direct Primary Care: An Innovative Alternative to Conventional Health Insurance," (The Heritage Foundation, Backgrounder # 2939 on Health Care, August 6, 2014), available at: http://www.heritage.org/research/reports/2014/08/direct-primary-care-an-innovative-alternative-to-conventional-health-insurance (Accessed 5/24/2015).

333 NCSL, "Mandated Health Insurance Benefits and State Laws: Updated & material added January 2014", available at, http://www.ncsl.org/research/health/mandated-health-insurance-benefits-and-state-laws.aspx (Accessed 1/23/2016).

334 George J. Annas, "The Baby K Case," *New England Journal of Medicine* 330: 1542-45 (1994).

335 Regina E. Herzlinger and Ramin Parsa-Parsi, "Consumer-Driven Health Care: Lessons from Switzerland," *JAMA* 292: 1213-20 (September 8, 2004), available at: http://bit.ly/YAS6ku. (Accessed 9/11/2014).

336 Raisa B. Deber, with Kenneth C. K. Lam, "Experience with Medical Savings Accounts in Selected Jurisdictions" (CHSRF [Canadian Health Services Research Foundation] Series of Reports on Financing Models: Paper 4, July 2011), available at: http://bit.ly/1qo9ioR. (Accessed 9/11/2014).

337 Avik Roy, "Obama Administration Denies Waiver for Indiana's Popular Medicaid Program," *Forbes*, November 11, 2011, available at: http://onforb.es/1gNeZ8o. (Accessed 12/15/2011).

338 Ibid.

339 Center on Budget and Policy Priorities, "Policy Basics: The Earned Income Tax Credit" (updated January 20, 2015), available at: http://www.cbpp.org/cms/?fa=view&id=2505. (Accessed 9/11/2014).

340 David Blumenthal, David Squires, The Commonwealth Fund Blog, "Do Health Care Costs Fuel Economic Inequality in the United States?", (September 9, 2014) available at: http://www.commonwealthfund.org/publications/blog/2014/sep/do-health-costs-fuel-inequality (Accessed 5/14/2015).

341 Health Insurance Portability and Accountability Act of 1996 (Public Law 104–191, 104th Congress), available at: https://www.gpo.gov/fdsys/pkg/PLAW-104publ191/pdf/PLAW-104publ191.pdf (Accessed 1/23/2016).

342 Chuck Marr and Chye-Ching Huang, "Misconceptions and Realities about Who Pays Taxes" (Center on Budget and Policy Priorities, September 17, 2012), available at: http://www.cbpp.org/cms/?fa=view&id=3505. (Accessed 9/11/2014).

343 U.S. Department of Health & Human Services, AHRQ (Agency for Healthcare Research and Quality). "The High Concentration of U.S. Health Care Expenditures" (Research in Action, Issue 19), available at: http://1.usa.gov/1lYBmOG. (Accessed 9/11/2014).

344 Herzlinger Regina, *Who Killed Health Care?: America's $2 Trillion Medical Problem – And The Consumer – Driven Cure,* McGraw-Hill, New York,2007, Part III p. 157-247

345 Christopher Koopman, Thomas Stratman, MohamedElbarasse, Mercatus Center, George Mason University, "Certificate-of-Need Laws: Implications for Michigan", (May 2015) available at http://mercatus.org/publication/certificate-need-laws-implications-michigan (Accessed 10/6/2015).

346 Sally Pipes, "The Way Out Of Obamacare", January 11, 2016, available online at, http://www.forbes.com/sites/sallypipes/2016/01/11/the-way-out-of-obamacare/ -2715e4857a0b937c0bc1ff48 (Accessed 1/24/2016).

347 Susan Dorr Goold and Mack Lipkin, Jr., "The Doctor-Patient Relationship: Challenges, Opportunities, and Strategies," *Journal of General Internal Medicine* 14 (supplement 1): S26-S33 (1999), available at: http://1.usa.gov/1BvBYij. (Accessed 9/11/2014).

348 Jason Fodeman, "The New Health Law: Bad for Doctors, Awful for Patients" (Institute for Health Care Consumerism), available at: http://bit.ly/1tNTBIW. (Accessed 9/1/2014).

349 EHR Incentives & Certification, "Meaningful Use Definition & Objectives," HealthIT. gov, http://bit.ly/1nORGgg (Accessed 9/11/2014).

350 University of Wisconsin, Population Health Sciences, "Improving Population Health: What Is Population Health?" available at: http://bit.ly/1CXl4ut. (Accessed 5/22/2015).

351 U.S. Food and Drug Administration, "Med Watch: The FDA Safety Information and Adverse Event Reporting Program," available at: http://www.fda.gov/Safety/MedWatch/ (Accessed 5/22/2015).

352 David C. Goodman and Elliot S. Fisher, "Physician Work Force Crisis? Wrong Diagnosis, Wrong Prescription," *New England Journal of Medicine* 358: 1658-61 (2008).

353 John C. Goodman, *Priceless: Curing the Healthcare Crisis* (Oakland, CA: The Independent Institute, 2012), Chapter 11, pp. 171-88.

CPSIA information can be obtained
at www.ICGtesting.com
Printed in the USA
FSOW02n2130150417
33066FS

9 780997 151121